COLIN & JUSTIN'S
HOW NOT TO
DECORATE

BRITISH BOARD OF BAD TASTE

COLIN & JUSTIN'S HOW NOT TO DECORATE

Certificate Argh!

COLIN McALLISTER
DESIGN GURU

JUSTIN RYAN
DESIGN GURU

This book may contain scenes of violent, clashing colours
and disturbing shell ornaments. This book may contain strong language,
as Colin and Justin confront yet another design nightmare.

This book has been certified as suitable for children as well as adults:
they have to learn design skills somewhere, and, let's face it, you lot are no help.

COLIN & JUSTIN'S
HOW NOT TO
DECORATE

TIME WARNER
BOOKS

TIME WARNER BOOKS

First published in Great Britain in November 2005 by Time Warner Books

Text copyright © Colin McAllister and Justin Ryan 2005

Format, Title and Other Material Copyright © Ricochet 2005

Photos copyright © Tom Howard
Additional photos from Five's *How Not To Decorate* TV series
© Matt Squire, Christopher Ridley and C Brendon Kelly/UNP

A CIP catalogue record for this book
is available from the British Library.

ISBN 0 316 73199 4

Designed and typeset by Smith & Gilmour, London
Printed and bound in Great Britain by The Bath Press

Time Warner Books
An imprint of
Time Warner Book Group UK
Brettenham House
Lancaster Place
London WC2E 7EN

www.twbg.co.uk

Dedicated to the hopeless and hideous homes of Great Britain. Without you we're nothing.

'One day, within our lifetime, we will have touched the glamour brush across every property in Great Britain.'
Justin Ryan, the Winston Churchill of Fabulous Design

CONTENTS

COLIN McALLISTER

Colin McAllister is the *nosiest* person in Britain. A seasoned curtain-twitcher, his interest in other people's homes started at the tender age of five, when he realised he could see into neighbouring properties from the comfort of his own bedroom. He soon established a merciless tick list of designer dos and don'ts, which begs the question – was it because of nosey parkers like Colin that many local houses began sporting what he now calls 'the multiple window treatment'?

'Why, oh why?' asked the young Mr C, did his neighbours feel the need to have blinds, curtains AND nets obscuring the view from each property porthole? And why, for that matter, did the people opposite have prints of small boys with huge, tear-filled eyes? And why did that oriental lady have such a green complexion? And just who *were* the naked couple seeking sanctuary on the wings of a giant swan?

As the eighties rolled forward, Colin's teenage years were a time of experiment and discovery, as a spotty, gangly 'Goth' discovered the thrill of an all-black wardrobe and the doom-laden sounds of Soft Cell, Theatre of Hate and Alien Sex Fiend. Not to mention the joy of having a bedroom painted entirely deep purple.

Changing sartorial direction on the merest whim, the teenage Colin bounced like a silver pinball from one style to another, with more costume changes than Liberace. And, boy, did he cover some ground! Think mod revival (tweed jackets and desert boots) new romantic (Adam Ant make-up and Bowie trousers) and finally his life-long passion: DISCO – sadly *without* the glitter boob tube and stack-heeled boots. As fashion styles changed, so too did his interior direction and the deep purple of his bedroom suddenly gave way to an all-white then all-black scheme and then eventually to a dramatic Moroccan look.

After Colin and Justin met in 1985, the dynamic duo moved into rented accommodation and were able to style their first project together – their own home. And, cash-strapped though they were, they did it without breaking the bank. Charity shops, flea markets and rubbish skips were regularly plundered as discarded wardrobes became painted armoires and flooring planks became funky suspended shelving.

Several properties later, passion became trade and the boys moved into home-interest journalism via *Livingetc* and *Good Homes* and then broadcasting via the BBC's *Trading Up* and *Million Pound Property Experiment*. And, of course, *How Not To Decorate* on Five … It's been a busy time, but Colin's job has only just begun. As far as he's concerned, the nation's homes are still in peril. Thank God he has the cure!

PS He's still twitching his curtains, only now they're 100 per cent New Zealand wool bouclé with a wonderful velvet trim …

'Mr Mac is perfectly happy to muck in, even during a spot of demolition DIY, as long as there's an open-nail surgeon standing by, ready to deal with any talon trauma that could occur ...' Justin on Colin

JUSTIN RYAN

Hailing from Fort William, Scotland, Justin discovered interior design at an early age; in fact, even before high school, he was style *obsessed*. Blessed with parents who favoured elegant schemes, he was nevertheless allowed to indulge his flamboyant sense of colour in his own bedroom.

Ironically, it was this very freedom that taught restraint. *Aye*, after lime-green, khaki and black schemes had all been tried, he soon found that less is most *definitely* more. By his teens, Justin had tried it all in his bedroom. Oh, *yes* – he'd sponged, rag-rolled and colour-washed *everything* except the carpet. He'd made the joyous journey from 'junk to funk' with a million curio shop finds and, via countless items pulled from skips, he'd made 'trash to treasure' a veritable art form. Blimey – this boy had vision . . .

At seventeen he moved to Glasgow where the ball *really* started rolling. Indeed, while studying psychology at Glasgow University it soon transpired that the local auction rooms held more appeal than his lecture rooms. Before long, the mechanics of the human brain took second place to glossy home interiors. Justin's fascination with design continued to grow and soon he was invited to appear on a Scottish TV programme called *The Home Show*. While others might have been delighted with that career peak, the young Mr R saw an opportunity. Turning his 'moment' into a ten-minute show reel (with the addition of a song and jazz-handed dance routine – *don't* ask: it was intended to

show 'versatility') – he hounded TV companies . . . refusing to take no for an answer.

Anyway – to cut a long story short, an early journalistic career blossomed. Pooling resources with his partner Colin, Justin counted time until, like a bolt of designer lightning, it happened. Auntie Beeb (having sighted the aforementioned *very* showbizzy show reel) suggested a screen test in Birmingham. A pant-wettingly scary audition followed (where J and C turned an old wine box into a funky medicine cabinet), after which the boys expected to hear nothing.

Justin still winces as he recalls the look on the director's face and prays to this day that the evidence will be forever lost in the annals of BBC Brum. But fortune, as they say, favours the brave. That same wincing director spied potential and, before long, a vertiginous ascent had begun. Several series of *Trading Up* and *Housecall* followed, as did the controversial *Million Pound Property Experiment* (a project that resulted in J and C gifting £275,000 profit to Children in Need), before the lads moved to Five to front *How Not To Decorate* and *The Farm*.

Sometimes Justin wishes he had taken his psychology studies to a higher level. Then he might understand why the people of Britain are so obsessed with stencilling, rag-rolling and the collecting of gonks. Is half of Britain certifiable on the grounds of design insanity? Judging by what Colin and Justin have witnessed, that would be an understatement . . .

‘Darling, Justin doesn't like to paint anything! The only thing he paints is his tan on. Every bloody morning ... ’ Colin on Justin

INTRODUCTION

'WE SCARE...

C'mon guys – admit it. You've flicked through this book and now you've got a migraine. 'I know how to decorate,' you thought to yourself. 'I'll just browse through this for a superior snigger.' Well, we've caught you!

We bet you're looking round your less-than-des res with a mixture of shock and horror. Is it any wonder that you're eyeing your comedy pig collection and wincing with guilt? Or looking at your shag pile bathroom carpet and thinking, TOXIC!

But panic not – Uncle Colin and Uncle Justin are here to help. Let us show you how to ditch those mismatched patterns and over-swagged curtains and demand instead a gorgeous world where everything is *fabulous*. A world where good taste triumphs over bad. And while we're at it, let us make you a better person, by design, so YOU can learn How NOT To Decorate. Aye – read it and reap, darlings, read it and reap!

So; bad taste...it's a disease. And a scary one at that. You've got woodchip in the bathroom and carpet in the kitchen. You've clad your living-room walls with fake stone to accommodate that even faker electric fireplace (the one with the spinning disc that, ahem, 'replicates' real flames) and you've invested in a shell-shaped sofa and a whisper-pink bath. Hmm. It's not looking good. You're suffocated by smoked-glass display cabinets and your pine furniture is so orange it makes Justin's fake tan look positively restrained. Your dreaded, sorry, *leaded* glass windows are a pane in the designer butt and your swagged and tailed curtains have, well, sagged and failed. Blimey – things are REALLY bad.

But hold on a sec – you're NOT alone! The whole country, it seems, is similarly afflicted; our shows are testament to that. Okay, it's been said that we get a bit gobby when we're out and about, but to put it simply – we *scare*...because we *care*. Indeed, *darlings*, where other style icons purr and soothe and tiptoe their way through home neglect, we go straight for the jugular. Every time.

...BECAUSE WE CARE'

But whoa! What gives us the right to battle home hell and scream from the rooftops about desperate dens? Allow us to elucidate – in a word, EXPOSURE. You see, Britain – as we know it – is steeped in a quagmire of design malaise, it is drowning in a bog of bad taste and strangled by its own swags and tails. In our travels we've seen hundreds of hideous homes, millions of miserable *maisons* and billions of bilious boltholes. It's too late for diplomacy: we're on the warpath!

We've witnessed a medieval fortress positioned twenty flights up a high-rise; we've experienced a Mexican bordello in a boxroom in Woking. Yes, we've been there and done that so you don't have to. So stick with us through this name and shame bible and learn ... by *other* people's mistakes. And all from the comfort of your own (soon to be improved) home.

So what's our strategy? Well, we're going to take you round a typical British home, room by room. It could be your parents' home. It could be a close friend's. Okay, let's not beat about the bush: it's probably YOUR home. And don't forget, this is an interactive book, so feel free to scream in horror and barf in disgust at the hideous design horrors that otherwise normal, reasonable British folk have inflicted on their poor, innocent abodes.

Remember our mantra: 'There are only two types of taste in this world – good and bad.' And let's face it, the former category belongs to us and the latter to everyone else. Which is why you need this fabulous book. More an indulgent celebration of bad taste than a glossy account of good, we hope it will steer you on the path to decorative self-improvement. Darlings, it's the perfect course of aversion therapy. Aye, our wee tome is a grizzly account of less than grand design, but we promise that by the closing chapter you'll have become a better and more stylish person in the process. Darlings, we're a pair of bad-taste-busting superheroes and we're on a mission! And that mission is to de-theme, de-clutter and de-uglify Britain's housing stock ... one dodgy property at a time. Looks like we're gonna be busy ...

'Is it a bird? Is it a plane? No, it's two designers with some socks stuffed down their pants.'

ARE YOU A DESIGNER DIVA . . .

**Ask yourself the following questions to find out
if you're challenging style or style-challenged!**

Avocado is seen at its best:
a) In a huge bowl of guacamole.
b) As an accent colour in a modern living room.
c) As a wonderful fitted bathroom suite complete
with gold swan taps and a bidet.

Texture is:
a) The new colour, darling!
b) The bobbles on an old throw that's been draped across
your sofa for years.
c) The woodchip wallpaper covering every wall in your home.

The best use for cork in the home is:
a) As a bottle stopper to stop your Beaujolais spilling
all over your new Habitat sofa.
b) As a fun and funky pin board in your kitchen, especially
if it's studded with brightly coloured pins.
c) As a splash-back around the edge of your sink and bath.

Kelly Hoppen is:
a) A Goddess! The former Interior Designer of the Year
and Queen of the East Meets West style.
b) Featured in a copy of *House & Garden* that you once
thumbed through at the dentist's.
c) The jolly bearded man who used to present *Stars
in Their Eyes*.

... OR A DESIGNER DODO?

No home should be without:
a) Colin and Justin's *How Not To Decorate*:
the modern design bible for every home in Britain.
b) At least two throws and four cushions.
c) A fluffy bathmat set, complete with a pee-stained
toilet rug.

Home is:
a) Where the Eames sofa is.
b) Wherever the television is.
c) Where the Artex is.

ANSWERS
Mostly a's: you have a tasteful, modern approach to home
styling and are an interior guru in the making.
Mostly b's: pretty hit or miss, aren't you? Successful home
style, as far as you're concerned, is more down to luck than
anything else.
Mostly c's: get thee to a church and repent for all the design
crimes you've committed over the years!

WEL

'This isn't a garden – it's the local landfill site after a herd of elephants has just trampled through it . . .'

There's always one that lets the side down, isn't there?
And yes, this really is the front of the house.

‘In their desperate attempts to turn trash to treasure, Colin and Justin even considered new careers as bin men.’

PAVEMENT PRESENCE

Pavement: (n) the strip of ground between your home and the road.
Presence: (n) the image your exterior conveys to other people.
Oh. My. God: (ph) exclamatory phrase used by frightened designers
    when confronted with another house of horror.

Before we step over the threshold, let's take a look at your exterior. If, that is, we can see past the overgrown hedge, the overstuffed bins, the over-the-top stone cladding and the jacked-up Ford Escort. You lot …

Ah – the great outdoors! For the love of God, you've GOT to sort out this mess! DON'T think that just because your gaff is gorgeous *inside* (hmm, even that's debatable – we'll get back to you shortly) that it negates what's going on *outside*. It *doesn't*! This is your shop window after all, so take a tip; at the very least … trim your bush! You owe it to yourselves AND your neighbours, who, take it from us, have been bitching about you all the way to the garden centre and back, thanks to your 'unconventional' approach to landscaping. And if you won't do it for them … then do it for us, 'cos we're the ones who have to deal with your fiendish frontages every time our cameras roll. And it ain't pleasant.

GRAB THE SICK BAG!

Quick, pass us the Pepto Bismol lest we lose our lunch. Is it any wonder we're gagging at the thought of all the things we've encountered on our travels around Britain?

 We've tiptoed through rockeries of pet excrement.

 We've cowered beneath mountains of abandoned washing machines, microwaves and rusting car parts.

 We've shrieked No No Noooo! to gnomes.

 We've winced over faux-Georgian pillared entranceways on three-bed Sutton semis.

 We've choked back the tears for brickwork hidden below inches of puke-inducing pebble dash.

So before you pick up the phone and invite us round for a cup of tea and a Jammie Dodger, ask yourself this question – would the entrance to your home make us want to jump with joy? Or jump off a cliff?

Aye, it's scary what some people have done to that small strip that marks out the approach to their home. We've seen exteriors that would make the Dingles blush. Derelict, bricked-up cars on the front lawn. Smashed-up baths blocking paths to front doors. Rubbish bags and litter build-up more reminiscent of a 1970s bin strike than a suburban sanctuary. But one of the external evils we most hate to encounter is ...

wait for it ...

big build-up ...

and then drum roll ...

...stone cladding!!

It leaves us reeling like Rottweilers licking cat pee off a nettle. Indeed, fake stone in *all* its myriad forms is an unsightly and hellish blight on perfectly good property. It devalues and demeans your home; after all, would you step out of the front door encased in pebbles? Enrobed in rocks? No, we didn't think so, so have some respect for your poor old house. Stoned? Well, you'd have to be to enjoy it.

Perhaps the most dramatic front folly we've ever seen is the Essex home of Sylvie and Eddie Rackham. Yup, bedded deep in the heart of Romford (an area that never fails to provide rich pickings for our TV shows) we stumbled upon a home exterior so OTT that we stopped dead in our tracks. A hellish hoopla of sculpted brick and concrete, it 'jumped' from the road like an explosion in a quarry, and as we talked and baulked with its 'designers' we discovered something incredible. Believe it or not, it was featured in the *News of the World* back in 1974 as – get this – a seriously STYLISH house, to which readers should aspire! You could have knocked us down with a Marabou feather. How times (THANK GOD) have changed.

Yabadabado?

Now that's how to make an entrance.

What we never quite understood about Sylvie and Eddie's home is why it never changed as the decades rolled forward. After all, they changed their clothes, their car, they chose different holiday destinations every year because they liked to experiment. But when it came to their house – and we're talking inside and out – they abandoned all sense of right and wrong and let time stand still.

'Write it out a hundred times: stone cladding is evil, stone cladding is evil, stone cladding is evil...'

WINDOWS AND DOORS

Once you've beaten your way through the front jungle, past the woodland creature statues and on to the crazy-paved path, you'll find that the next offender, in many homes, is the front door. This normally comes in one of two vile varieties: the dirty and derelict front door OR the overblown, NOT so grand, entrance!

Derelict doors

 Rusty letterboxes – that either don't flap at all or have the flap missing. Lovely. Why not just stick up a sign saying 'we don't give a toss'?

 Cat doors – we've seen front doors with proper cat flaps, but we've also seen doors with socking great holes cut into them, just so Mr Tibbles can stroll in whenever he fancies. Either way they look terrible, so pop them to the rear.

 Peeling and flaking paint – makes your door look like it's been on a two-week package holiday to Ibiza without any sun cream. It screams neglect and is SO not a good look.

 Broken windowpanes – inexcusable! And the solution to this – surprise, surprise – a new window. Not cardboard and Sellotape.

 Litter build-up – yup, the whirlwind of crisp packets and coke cans strewn across your front porch really makes a great first impression. Not.

Not So Grand Entrances

 Doors with double D brass knockers – whacking great knockers may look fab on Abi Titmuss but they look tacky, tacky, tacky on your front door.

 Doorbells that play the 'Birdie Song' or 'Greensleeves'. Aaarghhh!

 Overblown name signs. Giant nameplates are way over the top. And who are you expecting to read your name tag, anyway? Fly-past fighter pilots?

 Overuse of stick-on stained-glass panels and leafy frosted designs. They are gaudy and *way* too much.

 Chronic colours – bubble-gum pink and lime-green do NOT make good front door colours. Opt instead for something that's in keeping with the style of your house – black, Racing Green and Oxford Blue all work well.

 UPVC doors on a period property are plastic UNfantastic.

 Similar rules apply to the care and presentation of windows, although the most important thing about them is that they should be clean. So wield the soapy water and then buff up your panes until they shine. Doing this will give your house an instant facelift.

Ditch your good-for-nothing garden with Colin and Justin's Classic Tips

Stone-cladders Sylvie and Eddie are not alone in failing to make that vital first impression. With a little more thought about pavement presence, half of Britain's homes could be improved overnight. Just imagine!

 Weed is good – yup, weed your plot. It ain't rocket science, sweet cheeks, so ditch the dandelions ...

 Up the garden path – make sure your walkway is clear of rubbish and overgrown plants – unless you want friends to fall on their arses when they visit. Actually, in some cases that's not such a bad idea ...

 Trim your bush – give your greenery a horticultural Brazilian to make it appear tidier and more orderly.

 Windows are a pane – so clean them! Grubby glass not only looks dodgy from the outside but blocks out up to 20 per cent of natural light on the inside too. But remember to install curtains or blinds: you don't want the rest of your street seeing through your newly cleaned windows and spotting your fella chasing you around in the buff!

 Make an entrance – paint your front door and window frames. Some elbow grease (the kind you won't find bottled at B&Q) and a swift coat of paint will joosh up your approach like lippy and eyeliner on a tired fizzog.

 Stash the trash – if you can, hide your bin at the back of your house or behind a timber screen: who wants to see your rubbish when they call by? Quite.

Put a lid on it! There's
no excuse for ignoring
these pointers.

 Say it loud and say it proud! – ensure your number or nameplate can be clearly seen; a little confident signage never did any harm and it helps you relocate your own home when you've had a night on the bubbly, darling. But remember what we said before: not *too* OTT or it will look tacky even when you're DRUNK.

 Chip off the old block – ditch the stone cladding and peel off the pebble dash – they're ugly and fooling nobody. And get rid of that crazy paving … it's so NOT cool these days. Come to think of it, it never was.

 Gnome sweet gnome – lose the little plaster of Paris imps cluttering up your frontage. And while you're at it ditch the wagon wheels, the wind chimes, and anything else you can buy for 25p from a car boot sale.

 Pampas grass is crass – lonely single Pampas bush sticking out of your lawn? Now, let's be serious: you know it looks naff. At the very least plant around it to make it look less plonked or, better still, move it somewhere a little more discreet. Like into the bin you've just moved out of sight.

You could follow most of these tips in a single weekend and transform your execrable entrance from hellish to heavenly. What else were you planning to do with your time, anyway? Stick some louvre doors on to the outside of your home and pretend they're window shutters? Make a night light out of a perforated bean can? The devil will find work for idle decorating hands …

2 Hideous Hallways

HIDEOUS HALLWAYS

Okay – you've made it, eyes popping in horror, past that disastrous front garden. You've shut the door behind you with an audible sigh of relief. And then you see it – the hallway of horror for which no one could have prepared you. It's a tiny area (the average British hall measures approximately 3.5 x 5 feet) and *everything* is going on. Daylight is obscured by a heavily curtained window and a carpet so dark, worn and light-absorbing that it sends a gloomy chill round the minuscule space. God alone knows why the owners painted it such a revolting colour, and God only knows why they chose to do the woodwork in bright green gloss. And don't get us started on the cartoon cutouts made from polystyrene tiles. What, you think we're making this up? We wish . . .

'DEMONIC DECOR AHEAD!
Hide behind the sofa, look through your hands or pop on your Gucci shades before turning the page. In fact, do all three 'cos this one is SCARY . . . '

WHEN GOOD HOMES GO BAD #1
STAIRWAY? IT'S MORE LIKE A SCAREWAY...

We were speechless (yes, US – *speechless*) when we walked into this awful wee space. Our eyes hung out on stalks and our stomachs leapt. What in the name of all that's tasteful was going on here? Our guilty homeowners told us they were looking for their 'inner child'. Take it from us; if this was a child then it'd be hanging around street corners in a shell suit. Clutching an ASBO...

Question – What do you think when you look at this picture?

a) It's gorge – you see, I'm mad, me, and that's exactly how I'd like my hallway to look...

b) I can see what they're getting at although it might not be to everyone's taste...

c) I quite like the colour scheme but I'm not sure about the carpet and the stick-on animals...

d) OH MY GOD – there are some seriously mental people out there... that whole scheme is absolutely gross!

Answer – there is really only one. And, come on guys: as open-minded as we know you are – it's d. Yup – you'd be nuts to think there was any other response. We mean, please! That carpet, those stick-on animals, that glossy green woodwork. Must we continue?

' Panic over! Turn the page for some sweet relief ... '

Thank God we passed through Eastbourne when we did, otherwise this grown-up couple might have been forever lost, swimming in a sea of bizarre bad taste and bunny pee. We MIGHT have understood the junior attempt at colour coordination if they had children, but the only patter of tiny feet in this household came via the half-dozen or so rabbits that ran freely around the place.

Thankfully, the design remedy was easy – if ripping it all out and starting again can be called easy. The key to using colour successfully is to know where to start ... and, of course, when to stop. We painted the walls softest almond, the banister satin white (to cover that AWFUL yellow woodwork) and we added a mustard carpet. Thoroughly neutralised, we introduced shots of colour by hanging long timber boards painted with a jaunty orange and yellow barcode. And then, just because we could, we commissioned stained-glass windows and banister panels to match. The look was sympathetic to the owners' love of colour, but WITHOUT looking like the set of *Teletubbies*. We think the results speak far more than words ever could. But we'll leave you with one – GORGEOUS. Job done.

'That highway to hell is now a stairway to heaven. Simply divine.'

WHEN GOOD HOMES GO BAD #2
HOW NOW BROWN COW? QUITE.

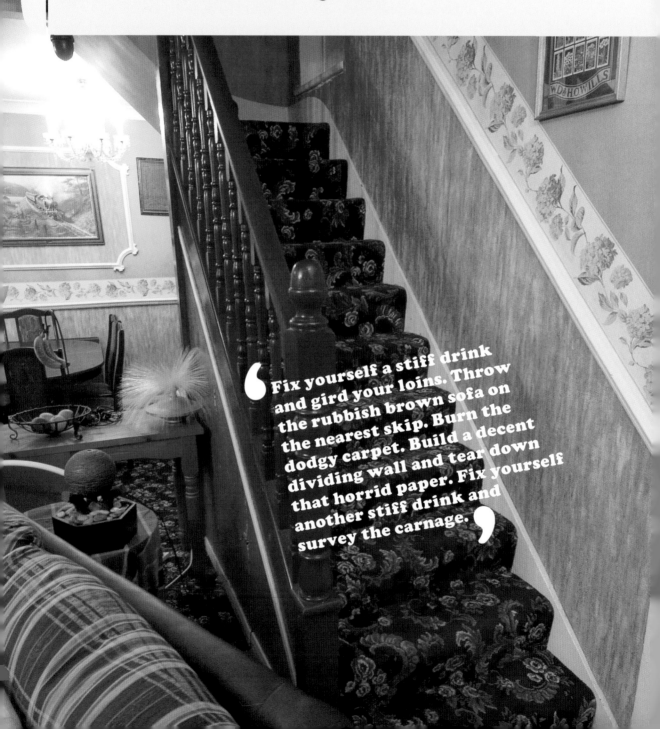

‘Fix yourself a stiff drink and gird your loins. Throw the rubbish brown sofa on the nearest skip. Burn the dodgy carpet. Build a decent dividing wall and tear down that horrid paper. Fix yourself another stiff drink and survey the carnage.’

'When suitably calmed, paint everything cream and add neutral carpet. Gosh, lovely Ann Maurice would be SO proud . . .'

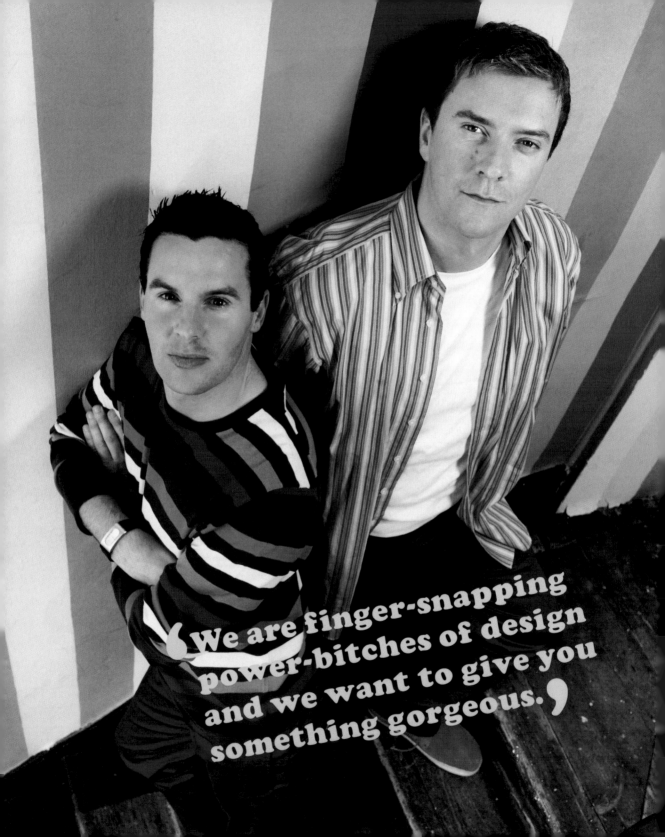

‘We are finger-snapping power-bitches of design and we want to give you something gorgeous.’

In our travels we've come across a zillion things that clutter up the nation's entranceways and ruin that vital first impression. In fact the average British hallway has more in common with Steptoe and Son's junkyard than a friendly space where you can greet your guests. True, a lot of homes have narrow hallways where there isn't room to swing a cat (which we wouldn't recommend anyway – your poor moggy is probably traumatised enough by your appalling decor). But a bad designer blames his space; after all, narrow corridors can look just fabulous when well put together – it's all the junk that fills them that we have a problem with. The ones we see are cluttered up with bicycles, stacks of old newspapers and free sheets, coat stands, broken lawn mowers and a million and one boxes of household junk that should have been ditched ages ago. As we've said a million times before, 'you only get one chance to make a good first impression', so don't waste it.

There are loads of simple things you can do to make your hallway better, and if you've been watching our shows you'll already be conversant with our ideas. If you've been channel hopping (you dirty dogs) then you might need a few reminders to help you get it right at, ahem, point of entry. Dear God – we're like a pair of old agony aunts … Anyway, listen up. Here goes.

J AND C'S CLASSIC HALLWAY TOP TIPS

 Clear out all the crap – face it, your hallway is messy and it's little more than a passage to other rooms. There's no excuse for this – get it sorted.

 Ask your friends. Then ask them again – most British halls are tiny, and your choice of decor can make or break the entire look. Ask your most honest friend (the one that tells you where you've got cellulite and buys you deodorant for Christmas) for their opinion. Chances are they'll say something like, 'Oh, it's not that bad', but they're just being kind. To get the real truth, pin them to the ground and throw pepper in their eyes until you hear the words '…you ought to be ASHAMED…I've never seen anything so PUTRID…it's a DISGRACE.' Only then will you realise that your hallway is hellish to the power of ten million.

 Size matters – if your hall is a tall, skinny fellow then cut him down to size! Divide the wall height by three, and then a third of the way from the floor whack on a budget timber picture rail (most DIY stores sell them for a couple of quid a metre). Slap on paint above the rail in a shade or two darker than the colour below. A classic technique that will make a BIG difference.

 Walk tall – if you have the opposite problem, i.e. a low ceiling, then cheat your way to success! Trick the eye into thinking the walls are taller by choosing a vertical striped paper. Darlings, it's a doddle! An even cheaper way is to use masking tape and paint to create your own stripes.

 Tunnel vision – if your hall's more like a never-ending tunnel than a warm, homely space then take our advice and foreshorten it by painting the end wall a darker shade. Conversely, for a wee squat corridor paint the end wall a lighter shade to help stretch things forward.

Less is more – minimise to maximise! Opt for one or two key pieces of artwork rather than cluttering up walls with loads of smaller images. This frees up eye lines and makes limited space feel more abundant.

 Hoof it – hallways take heavy traffic so opt for hardwearing carpets. And plonk a big mat inside your front door for a final wipe before going further inside, remembering to clean it regularly. (Yes, we know we sound bossy but we only want to help you.)

 Striptease – a sartorial dressing down will help you streamline, so hang coats, jackets and umbrellas out of sight in the area under the stairs or in a shallow cupboard that doesn't eat greedily into your walkway.

 Times table – if your hallway's wide enough, then add a narrow console table, dress either side with tall lamps and position a piece of artwork above to provide impact. Doing this promotes an immediate welcoming feel when guests enter your home.

 Pull up a chair – if you've got room for a comfy seat and a small side table then create instant mood by setting up a little zone that can double as somewhere to take phone calls etc.

 Cover up – unsightly radiators will look much better with a slick cover (try Jali or Argos – see Selected Resources, p. 248). Make them a feature by dressing the wall above with a large piece of framed art.

 Hall of mirrors – double the perceived space by using large mirrors to reflect light. If you want to create an infinity effect, position mirrors directly opposite each other. Go easy on the bevy before glancing at your image – it can be very dizzying to see yourself a hundred times over, unless, of course, you're as gorgeous as us!

3 Lurid Living

Rooms

'Fake tan, fake fur, but honey: the rest is all real'

Damn it – you're strong. You can cope with this carnage. Just prepare yourself, that's all we ask. Pause for a moment. Take a deep breath. Are you ready yet? Good. Here goes.

You've left behind that hallway of horror but now you're feeling *really* nervous. There's a doorway to the left and you can hear the rumbling blast of a television set. You look down and through a crack in the door you can see the beginnings of a swirling, pub-style carpet. Your stomach churns. Oh dear ... Are you ready to push open the door and walk towards what lies beyond?

Darlings, we've seen it all. Like a pair of property Poirots, we've crawled our way round the UK's worst lounges in search of *extreme* design trauma. And did we find it? Well, what do *you* think? OF *COURSE* WE DID.

'I think I detect pussy'

Colin prays for world peace and an end to woodchip wallpaper.

In fact, we should be given medication after some of the things we've seen. This chapter, a name and shame account of British lounges, will, if nothing else, leave you bent over the bog losing last night's curry while baying at the moon in decorative horror. And just try doing both those things at the same time – it gets VERY messy.

Anyway, you should know that writing this section was a deeply traumatic experience. We had to search back into our repressed memories and remind ourselves of all the disturbing things we'd seen on our travels. Only then could we pinpoint all the evil elements that conspire to make a truly, madly, deeply, deadly living room. Ah well, even we need some aversion therapy now and then.

The root of the problem is the way in which Britain goes about styling its living rooms. Okay, in the past there wasn't as much reference material available, but in this modern day and age – with tons of technology at our fingertips and a world of designer stores, TV shows and magazines available to plunder – there is NO excuse for getting it so wrong. You just have to look at the TV schedules to see what we mean. And you just have to scan the row upon row of home titles in newsagents up and down the land. Then there are the shops, the DIY stores and events such as the *Daily Mail* Ideal Home Show, which bend over backwards to make Britain style literate. The clues are all out there but it's up to you to make the most of them. If you don't, your living rooms will always look like the ones you see here.

'Sorry love, the stone age look went out with the dinosaurs.'

WHEN GOOD HOMES GO BAD #3
STONE ME!

Can you spot the six home horrors in this, ahem, 'living' room??

1 The padded velour sofa that has all the allure of a pound of liverwurst.

2 The scandalous faux stonework fireplace that's actually just plaster and paint.

3 The frilly-topped pink velour curtains.

4 That gruesome coffee table.

5 The dodgy wallpaper.

6 The pawnshop-style ceiling light – that not even the pawnshop would want to buy.

This living room will be forever etched in our minds as one of the most ABSURD attempts at interior design we have ever seen. Come on! You've got to admit that it's just bizarre. Style issues aside, the family who lived there were actually rather normal and perfectly pleasant and we never quite got to the root of what possessed them . . .

However, as much as we remember this room as one of the worst we've ever tackled, we also remember that we were particularly overjoyed with 'the reveal'. Our wonderful builders (bless them!) had their work cut out, but followed our instructions to the letter and removed the fireplace and indeed everything else, from the striped wallpaper to that dated poo-coloured ceiling treatment. (Hmm, as if poo was *ever* in fashion.) In fact, spurred on by the promise of an Indian takeaway and a keg of Stella at the end of their shift, they emptied the room of all its dreadfulness faster than you can say 'chicken tikka masala'.

'Colin and Justin enter their blue period . . .'

God we LOVE this room! And, yes, we know self-praise is to be avoided, but we can't help ourselves. With the walls plastered smooth by our team, we painted most areas duck-egg blue but decided that breast would be best for the wallpaper. We raided B&Q for some gorgeous Tate Range paper and invested just £20 a roll. Ah, the joys of knowing *how* to decorate . . . and how to spend the dosh. Next we added a modern, electric, wall-hung fireplace and some chunky floating shelves. Then a spot of solid beech flooring and a pair of new sofas. Oh, and a chunky timber coffee table.

And let us tell you a secret. The owners of this house have 'a small rental property portfolio' (their words, not ours – we'd call them landlords). They delightedly explained that they planned to re-use everything we had discarded in one of their apartments. For the love of God! Let's hope they're paying the tenants to live there, and not the other way around. It's only fair.

'Rejoice and give thanks – it's a design miracle!'

Carpets

This touchy-feely feast for the footsies should be short-piled, devoid of pattern and generally 'self-coloured' – that's design speak for 'one shade covers all'. And, for crying out loud, you can forget 'sculpting', 'shading' or 'textured veining'. Opt for neutral colours so you can easily change your scheme further down the line and look at hardwearing products from companies such as Allied, Kersaint Kobb or Crucial Trading. Natural floor coverings such as coir or sea grass can look great and are certainly hardwearing, but get them wet? They smell like cat pee. Nice. So opt instead for a good wool and nylon mix that has all the look of natural but with a less odorous side effect. You have been warned …

Rugs

If you glance at a few of our 'after' shots, you'll see we're
rather partial to a nice rug. Again, self-coloured is best
or make sure any extra colours you do introduce match
the accent colours in the rest of the room. Oh – and this
may be a no no peculiar to us, but we can't get to grips
with the idea of rugs on rugs, i.e. 'double layering'.
On timber, oh yes ... but on yer Berber? Bugger off!!

Sofas and armchairs

Ditch anything shell-backed, lose the velour and FORGET pattern! Plastic swirly-looking 'timber' detailing at the arms and feet is criminal and, as for a combination of all these aspects – NOOOOOOOOOOOOO!!!!!!

   Opt instead for self-coloured fabric, comfy chunky shapes that will take the rough and tumble of everyday life and modern low-slung designs. Soft greys, taupes and creams work well but make sure you choose models that have removable and washable covers. You don't need an explanation – you know it makes sense. Sofa Workshop, Viva Sofas and George Maxwell are some of our favourites. Check the suppliers list at the end of our book for details.

Furniture

Britain has a fondness for flat-pack and, we suppose, nothing is ever going to change that. Don't get us wrong: it's not that we don't like the stuff (everything starts life as an assembly of component parts, after all – it's just that some furniture arrives READY assembled), more that we can't be bothered with the hassle of putting it all together. All that fumbling about with a forest of chipboard, bags of screws and an Allen key can be *very* disturbing. They say you should never be taught to drive by someone you love – it only leads to trouble – and the same applies to furniture assembly. As much as you try, you'll always end up putting the drawers in upside down and before you know it you're having a domestic.

Flat-packs aside there are a load of deadly design crimes played out on a daily basis by misguided British homeowners. Here are just a few.

 Coffee tables should NOT be made from old boxes with dinner trays balanced dangerously on top. Or, for that matter, from giant bobbin-type cable reels painted bright, 'funky' colours.

 Contrary to popular belief, shelving systems made from bricks and scaffolding planks are NOT where it's at.

 Nor, for that matter, are TV units fashioned from old tea chests – even if you've 'discovered' that placing them on their side with the top to the back gives you a handy place to stash the video.

You've got to use your common sense, guys, and think before you buy. And it's not as if there's even a valid excuse for getting it wrong these days. There are plenty of affordable options on the high street, so spend a little time and invest in decent kit. Even Argos, Ikea and Tesco sell inspired ranges that cost far less than you'd think.

Or why not hit your local auction house and buy something with a little history? A gorgeous piece of time-worn oak, perhaps, or a reassuringly heavy hunk of marble on a wrought-iron frame. Yup, thirty quid will pay for plenty, so do yourself a favour and get that bidding hand waving frantically in the air.

Which reminds us! Exercise a little caution, make sure you know what you're bidding for and have a top price in mind so you don't get carried away in a bidding frenzy. Otherwise the same might happen to you as happened to us. Aye, US! Picture it: Surrey, winter 2004. We became caught up in the moment, sidetracked and confused by the hustle and bustle of a jam-packed sales room. And we ended up paying three hundred quid for a Smeg range that was still in its original packaging. A bargain, you might think (after all, they're at least a grand new), until you realise we'd got our tartan knickers in a twist over the lots. Oops. We thought we were bidding for a set of six original Robin Day chairs and a matching table. To this day we've still got that range in our garage. Ah well, we'll find it a good home in the future ...

'Less is more darling, less is more.'

WHEN GOOD HOMES GO BAD #4
LIVING ROOM OR LAUNDRETTE?

By opting for stripy wallpaper and fabrics, the villains behind this particular design crime hoped to create a look that said 'Georgian'. Georgian? To us, darlings, it's more George and Mildred. And we're LOVING that clever corner storage – that's so boxing clever.

Q: Can you spot the six home horrors in here?
A: What, only six? Okay, there are loads more but these are the worst ...

1 Ratty over-varnished floorboards.
2 Heavily patterned sofas that look as if they've been lying in the garden for months.
3 Washing everywhere. Dot Cotton would feel at home here.
4 Appalling brick-feature fireplace with red-stained timber top.
5 The widow's peak pelmet: created in the ninth circle of hell.
6 Boxes of rubbish and clutter EVERYWHERE. Remember our motto: if it's not practical or beautiful – GET RID OF IT!!

'Colin and Justin. Glamorising Britain one house at a time.'

'Honesty time, folks. The owner of this redesigned room gave us it in the ear for choosing a pale colour scheme for her living room. And she was disappointed with the flooring we chose for her new conservatory. She said it was wholly inappropriate for a family house. Can we just remind you that the "before" picture for this shot is the living room on the previous page? Some people. Give 'em an inch . . . and all of a sudden they're Anouska blinkin' Hempel. '

It always strikes us as strange that the term 'living room' is applied in so many of the homes we come across, because most of them actually verge on the opposite. Possessing all the allure of a morgue, many British 'living' rooms have an aura of foreboding that would leave Quincy prepping for a decorative postmortem. Most provide little more than a place to sit at the end of each working day and that, as far as we're concerned, is criminal.

Living rooms should provide a cool sanctuary from the outside world. They should be domains where we can escape the trials of everyday life. They should be chill-out rooms where we can forget all our cares and just unwind. But most of the living rooms we've seen have been about as relaxing as an operating theatre in the middle of Oxford Street. No wonder Britain's stress levels have gone through the roof.

FEROCIOUS FIREPLACES – THE FIRES OF HELL

Every room should have a strong visual focal point. It can be an interesting architectural feature, an attractive piece of art or even something that's a whole lot simpler – a fireplace. If you add the right fireplace to your scheme, you'll create immediate impact and style. And when it comes to moving on, a beautiful fireplace will be a key selling point.

Could it be any easier? No. So why, then, as we travel the length and breadth of Britain, are we forced, in our travels, to endure wall upon wall of horrible hearths? The answer's obvious: you're all clueless. There's only one thing for it: we're taking you on a tour of the seven deadly fireplace sins, so that you can learn to avoid the flames of decorative damnation. Blimey – we're not just saving your homes, we're saving your souls!

And okay, we've kind of gone to town on this section, but let's face it: the fireplace is the starting point for most people's living rooms. Get it right and you'll glow with success. Get it wrong and you'll burn in the fires of decorating hell for all eternity. Dramatic, us? Mais *oui*.

Pride:
an excessive belief in one's own abilities; the sin from which all others arise.

The poor, misguided couple who lived here positively glowed with pride at this stone(d) monstrosity. Thankfully, help was at hand, and we saved them with a cool new marble fireplace positioned further into the main part of the room.

‘And the sleek shall inherit the earth . . . Well, a beautiful new living room, anyway.’

Envy:
the desire for others' traits, status, abilities or situation.

These homeowners were deeply envious of people who lived in log cabins and so chose to 'get the look' with some fake timber-style particleboard and a rugged stone fireplace. What they neglected to notice was that there aren't that many log-cabin dwellers in suburban Northampton!

'Hey, we know real wood when we see it! And don't you just dig the new fireplace, complete with a timber mantelpiece and a wood-burning stove!'

Greed:
the desire for material wealth or gain, ignoring the realm of the spiritual.

'I must have trolls, I must have more . . . This willing sinner positively binges on creepy, plastic dolls, which she displays in a bulging bookcase, hiding the majestic fireplace that lies behind.'

'Hot stuff! This is the perfect solution: a modern firebox for a thoroughly modern room and another convert to our colourful cult!'

Lust:
an inordinate craving for the pleasures of the body.

Don't think that the phallic nature of this stone tower fireplace has escaped us. It hasn't. Men with huge, skyward rock structures in their rooms are obviously making up for something! And yes, we know we've shown you this room before but come on guys; can you blame us for revelling in it all again?

Anger:
the individual who spurns love and opts instead for fury.

Seeing a room like this actually makes us angry. Aarghh! Look at it: terrible sofa, terrible wallpaper, and oh that shocking fireplace! They don't come much more dowdy than this. Quick, bring us the hammer …

Talk about a religious experience … this room has been born again. Praise be!

Gluttony:

an inordinate desire to consume more than that which one requires.

The couple who lived with this fireplace were gluttons for punishment: they hadn't learnt by the example of other rooms they'd already tackled. We put them on a strict diet of designer goodies and their once-tired old fireplace is suddenly burning with new desire.

'Feast your eyes, darlings.
It's poptastic.'

Sloth:
the avoidance of physical or spiritual work.

The avoidance of work in this tawdry room is obvious. C'mon, how many of you live with terrible things that you know you should change? The owners of this hearth had been putting off change for years but when we arrived the past came back to haunt them. Good job we know a thing or two about exorcism ...

Okay, so it's hiding bashfully behind a beautiful chair, but this is now a working fireplace – and GORGEOUS to boot!

Now that you know how a simple element like the right fireplace can start you on the path to righteousness, why not sit down and ponder for a moment. On the day of designer reckoning will you repent and cast out the evil within … or will you burn in the fireplaces of hell for ever?

OKAY, SO IT'S A LIVING ROOM, BUT IT'S LIVING IN THE PAST . . .

So, dear army of design devotees – are you taking all this in? Are you feeling named and shamed? Stand in the middle of your own living room and ask yourself this question: how much of this do you recognise? Be honest! And just to check you really have been paying attention, have a look at the following three pictures and see if you can work out . . . which is the worst.

Is it:

a) Our Eastbourne living room? Take one Portakabin, paint it to look like the Incredible Hulk has just exploded in there and then add a shocking mud-coloured velour three-piece suite just for good measure.

b) Our Northampton living room with its, ahem, delightful timber panelling, Bulls Blood-coloured vinyl sofa and that gorgeous brick-effect fireplace?

c) Our Edinburgh living room with its . . . with its . . . no, sorry chaps, we just can't bring ourselves to verbalise this one. It's just TOO awful.

Answer – they are ALL as bad as each other. Now, let's move on . . .

WHEN GOOD HOMES GO BAD #5
SAMANTHA FOX – CELEBRITY LOUNGE LOSER

Okay, so she might have a crackin' pair of boobs, an alright voice and a chirpy Cockney sparrow demeanour, but Sam Fox's decorating taste is positioned somewhere ... in her cute wee posterior. Her living room is proof positive that bad taste transcends Joe Public to land squarely at the feet of celebrity. Utterly stuck in the past, *Chez* Fox was desperate. We could hardly believe what we were seeing: a scary Gothic-blue scheme and vile velveteen curtains like some clapped-out film star's frock. The sofas, by Sam's admission, were particularly foul (a relic from girlfriend Myra's previous home) and as for the light installation around the fireplace? Oh My God. We thought we'd died and gone to design purgatory. Now take a deep breath, remember what this pop-star living room WAS like, and turn the page ...

Could this lounge be any more 'rock star' appropriate? Sure, it was a MASSIVE job but damn – look at it now! Seamless white walls, a white-painted floor and a dreamy arrangement of white leather furniture create a cool sanctuary of tonal perfection. Carefully selected blood-red accessories and artwork provide contrast and Sam and Myra add all the extra colour required ... by simply living there. Fabulous.

WALL COVERINGS

Now this is a tricky area and time-sensitive to say the very least. Blimey – wallpaper goes in and out of style more often than we quaff champagne in The Ivy. And that's a VERY regular occurrence indeed. So if you reread this book in a few seasons' time, the rules could be entirely different. In essence – less is more. Subtle patterns are okay as entire wall coverings – if delicate pattern is your thing – but if you like to make a bolder statement, maybe with geometric or retro designs, then the old 'accent wall' principle rocks every time. Pick a wall (the one that holds the fireplace is generally best) and go to town. If you want to get the mood into the rest of your space, then isolate one or two colours that appear in the paper and use accessories in these same shades to pull the space together. Or choose the background colour and use this on other walls to create gorgeous unity. It's easy, sweeties, when you know how …

Woeful Wallpapers

Welcome to the less than wonderful world of woeful wallpapers. We've put together a catalogue of catastrophic coverings that must be avoided at all costs. Little more than bad taste on a roll, these uglies are the strips of Satan and should never, ever, be used to decorate your home. And what is it they say? That the trick to successful wallpapering is in the hanging? Well, if you ask us, someone should be hanged for producing this little lot ...

'That wallpaper is migraine inducing. And I'm not just talking about one of those headachey migraines. I'm talking flashing lights and full-on nausea ... '

1970s beige – the perfect paper for rogue landlords, school jotters and Jarvis Cocker. And yes, it probably does come smelling of wee . . .

Burgundy metallic – stripes are tricky at the best of times, but add a metallic sheen (which will brilliantly highlight all your little lumps and bumps) and you've really got a recipe for disaster. Misguided homeowners might think this paper looks regal . . . but to us it's more twenty Regal.

Miserable mock-marble – hmm! A marble finish that's warm to the touch and peeling at the edges? Well THAT sounds authentic. But hey – why not go the whole hog and use it to line your entire smallest room for instant Roman bathhouse appeal? Yes, that peeling effect after just one bath is guaranteed to get your toga in a tangle.

Hellish hessian – this was originally designed as a heavy dressing for surfaces in really bad nick and that's why every property developer who ever stripped off this horrible stuff probably took half the wall off with it. It ain't decor, guys, it's camouflage.

Cork – great for champagne bottles, lousy for walls. Textural and cushioning, this 1970s staple brings a padded-cell feel to any room. So if you feel like chucking yourself against a wall then this is the one for you. For all other sane people, cork is like the platform shoe. Best left in the 70s.

Wood-effect panelling – the look of a log cabin without harming a single tree, which is fab, 'cos we love nature, in spite of what it did to us! A great look if you're Grizzly Adams, forty floors up in a tower block. Or if you're trying to capture the feel of a greasy spoon chez vous. Yup, just rub it down with lard and beans and you're away . . .

Gold-mesh effect – ideal for 1980s Hollywood wives, this brash and glitzy paper looks terrific if you're Jackie Collins but abysmal if you're Michelle Collins. Guaranteed to make any room look like a giant foil-wrapped bar of chocolate. You'd have to be a right Wonka to want it.

Hot red flock – we'll have to be careful here as damask papers are making a bit of a comeback. But, come on – can you imagine a small, boxy living room completely covered in red flock from top to toe? And it managing NOT to look like a 1970s Indian restaurant? Nope, neither can we . . .

Anything peach – ah yes, *peach*. That offensively inoffensive shade for an army of uncertain decorators. Up and down the land scores of homeowners are bickering, unable to come to a sensible decision about what colour to paint their homes. And, sadly, they usually concur about one shade. Yup, you've guessed it – the big P. 'But, honey, we don't want magnolia again, we want to add colour . . .' Pause. 'Okay, baby, what about peach . . .?'

Football wallpaper – keep the colours on the field and leave your child's room alone. Think about it – you want the little darling to sit quietly and go to bed early, so you pop him into a fussy, gaudy shrine to an athletic and powerful sport. And then you wonder why your little angel's hyperactive . . .

Textured wall coverings – including that evil of all evils, WOODCHIP! STOP – if your walls are lumpy and bumpy don't disguise them. Employ a plasterer and fix them. The only good thing about textured wall coverings? Blind people can hate them too.

Borders – just who exactly invented the border? And why do we want to know? Because we'd like to take them ACROSS the border and leave them there, that's why. Oh, and how people *use* them. At best around dado and picture rail height and at worst around doorframes, plug sockets and light switches. Don't do it – they were crap then and they're crap now. So avoid them like the plague.

'We're not just changing rooms, we're changing lives.'

LIGHTING

Right, bright spark, get it right – or you might as well ditch all your other 'home work' down the designer drain. Yup, lighting is a make or break matter and will improve or detract from your scheme like nothing else. Hey – it's easy to add atmosphere at the flick of a switch but blimey – it's even easier to goof … BIG time.

As far as we're concerned, the most foolproof and hassle-free way to create sympathetic illumination is to employ what's commonly known as 'mood lighting'. So now you know. However (and it's a BIG however), going by some of the eccentric electric lights we've seen, this could be better referred to as 'bad mood' lighting … Aye, we've seen it all. But more of that later.

So, *mood lighting*. It does exactly what it says on the tin. It promotes mood – and atmosphere – in your home, by creating comfortably lit zones in a mix of clever and sympathetic combinations. This type of lighting comes via 'wall washers', side lights, table lights and standard lamps, or via discreetly positioned lighting behind sofas, tables or plants. You get the gist. Similar to 'pool' lighting, which creates individual pockets of light where you need it most; it's important to get it right.

COLIN AND JUSTIN'S GUIDE TO LIGHTS THAT MAKE YOU PRAY FOR A POWER CUT

 Big, lumpy, fiercely fringed, horrid florid 'standard lamps'.

 Triffids – as we call them. Aye, those horrid lumieres that look as if they've dropped out of the sky and landed on the set of a 1950s B movie.

 Novelty lamps – anything shaped like a duck or a crumpled carrier bag. And those awful Aphrodite-shaped lamps with wax droplets.

 Fluorescent strip lights – especially the ones with plastic covers that collect frazzled flies. A nice touch in the kitchen …

 Cupped hands holding illuminated globes.

 Plastic fake Tiffany lamps.

 Giant brass eyeball spots in the ceiling (especially when it's an orange pine timber ceiling).

 Picture lamps – including illuminated scenes of the Taj Mahal or Niagara Falls. Unless you're seriously kitsch, there is no way you can carry off this look. Note: kitsch is what middle-class people call their bad taste.

 Fake disco lights. We mean, come on. Why??? And who'd want to get down and boogie in your lurid living room anyway?

 Lights that double as ceiling fans. We'd always worry they'd collapse and decapitate someone. Not a good look …

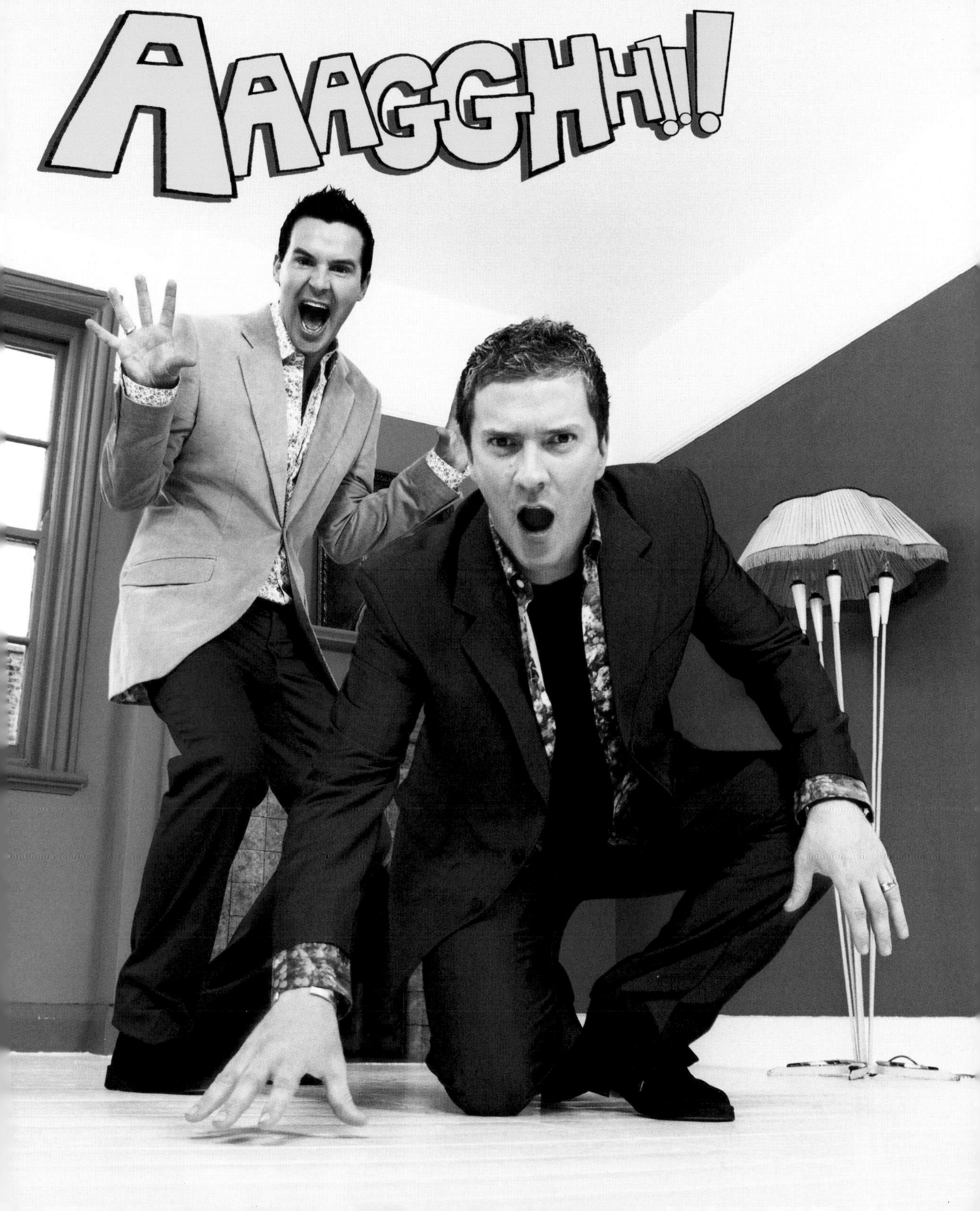
AAAGGHH!!!

Now that we've established the top ten lights to avoid, it's time to concentrate on the types you *should* buy. And, take it from us, twenty years in the business – man and girl – we know best.

Good lighting is so simple: just think elegant, understated and sophisticated. Like us. Well, maybe not the understated bit . . . or the sophisticated bit . . . or the elegant bit. But otherwise . . . snap! Even something as simple as a dimmer switch – which will only set you back a tenner – can make all the difference. If your living room looks like the Blackpool Illuminations, then twisting one of these wee fellows could make life a little less, well, in your face.

If you need a bit of inspiration, get yourself down town. In just a few short years the high street has gone from dull, dull, dull to actually rather *chi chi*, via a whole host of home-interest shops that have responded to the new style demands of Great Britain. These forward-thinking department stores and high street singles have upped the ante to the power of ten, and now carry stock collections that we thoroughly admire. Bhs have a particularly good department, as do Debenhams, M&S and House of Fraser, but this brings to mind one question: when sales of tasteful products are increasing all the time, why do we see so little of them in the homes we visit? Darlings, it's a mystery. But it's all got to be somewhere . . .

Other living room no nos

- Heavily textured ceilings – they look like meringue, but they're most definitely mer*wrong*. Leave the baked Alaska for the dinner table.

- Arrangements of dusty dried flowers in the fireplace. A log stack, yes, but a bunch of desiccated peonies? NO.

- Walls choked by that awful 1970s fake timber truck-stop panelling.

- Plastic plants and flowers – if you can't manage the real thing don't bother.

- Shell-backed sofas. (In fact, here's a tip: pretty much any 'style' item with the word 'shell' in it should be avoided. Shell-backed sofas, shell earrings, shell ornaments, shell suits … Shells look good on beaches. FULL STOP.)

- Swirly carpets. When you look at your floor, you should feel peaceful and rested, not as though you're on the new ride at Alton Towers.

- Cheap click-together laminate that has, ahem, unclicked. Who wants to see line after line of dusty cracks?

- Oversized TVs. Maybe it's just us but it seems that sofas are getting smaller and TVs are definitely getting bigger. What's going on?

- Cigarette-laden ashtrays lying everywhere. The smell, the look, the *eugh* …

CHRONIC COLLECTIONS

Just before we leave the now beautifully redecorated, calm and stylish living space and move on to the next room, let's take a moment to discuss something that can have a terrifying impact in every single room. In fact, when things go bad (and they always do) these can take over every single surface. If your house was a person (poor thing), then collections would be a very nasty rash that just spreads and spreads . . . Urgh!

So, with much fear and trepidation, let us enter the realm of the collector. Yup, that preoccupied individual who assembles objects with a similar theme for their interest, value or beauty. But be honest, are collections really worth collecting? Let's face it, most amount to pretty much nothing in terms of value, and the only thing that they gather . . . is dust. If you have to collect anything, then please keep it all to yourself. Arrange it in a discreet cupboard and don't let it overtake your life. If you can't fit it all in one cupboard . . . you have a problem, and need to contact Collectors Anonymous without delay.

Plates – these are for eating off and should come in a box with at least three others that match. They should not be emblazoned with pictures of horses or dogs or holiday destinations and they should never, ever, be hung on a wall. If you know someone with a plate collection, get a hammer and imagine yourself at a wedding. A Greek wedding …

Limited editions – if you own anything 'limited' to an edition of one million and mass produced in the Far East, you need help. And if you've 'invested' in an ultra-limited edition something-or-other bought at great expense in forty-three easy payments from the back of a Sunday supplement, you should be sectioned.

Ornaments – too many ornaments = complete and utter mess. Price is no indication of taste, so avoid expensive figurines: they're nothing more than posh clutter.

Model aircraft – why not hang your collection on fishing line from your bedroom ceiling? That way a few swipes with a handy shovel will end all your display worries.

Magazines – anyone who collects magazines is just asking for a house fire. Pile loads of paper around every inch of your home, add a smoking relative and just wait … And why would you want to read a magazine more than once in any case? Magazines are weekly and monthly for a reason: ditch them as soon as the new one is on the shelf.

Shoes/handbags – ooh, controversial. But no, no, no – girls! You really should know better. Here's a tip: every time you fancy buying your fiftieth pair of shoes, or your sixty-sixth handbag, put a fiver in the holiday fund. You'll be shaking your maracas in a sultry clime before you can say 'Blahnik'.

Watches – how many watches do you need? Do you really want all that time on your hands? Anyone who collects watches should be doing time, not collecting it.

Pigs/frogs/dogs/cats/cows – it's great to love animals, but don't go crazy. We love our cat Felix immensely but that doesn't mean we've filled our home with cat tea towels, cat mugs, cat figurines and furry cat slippers. If you love pets then show it with the real thing.

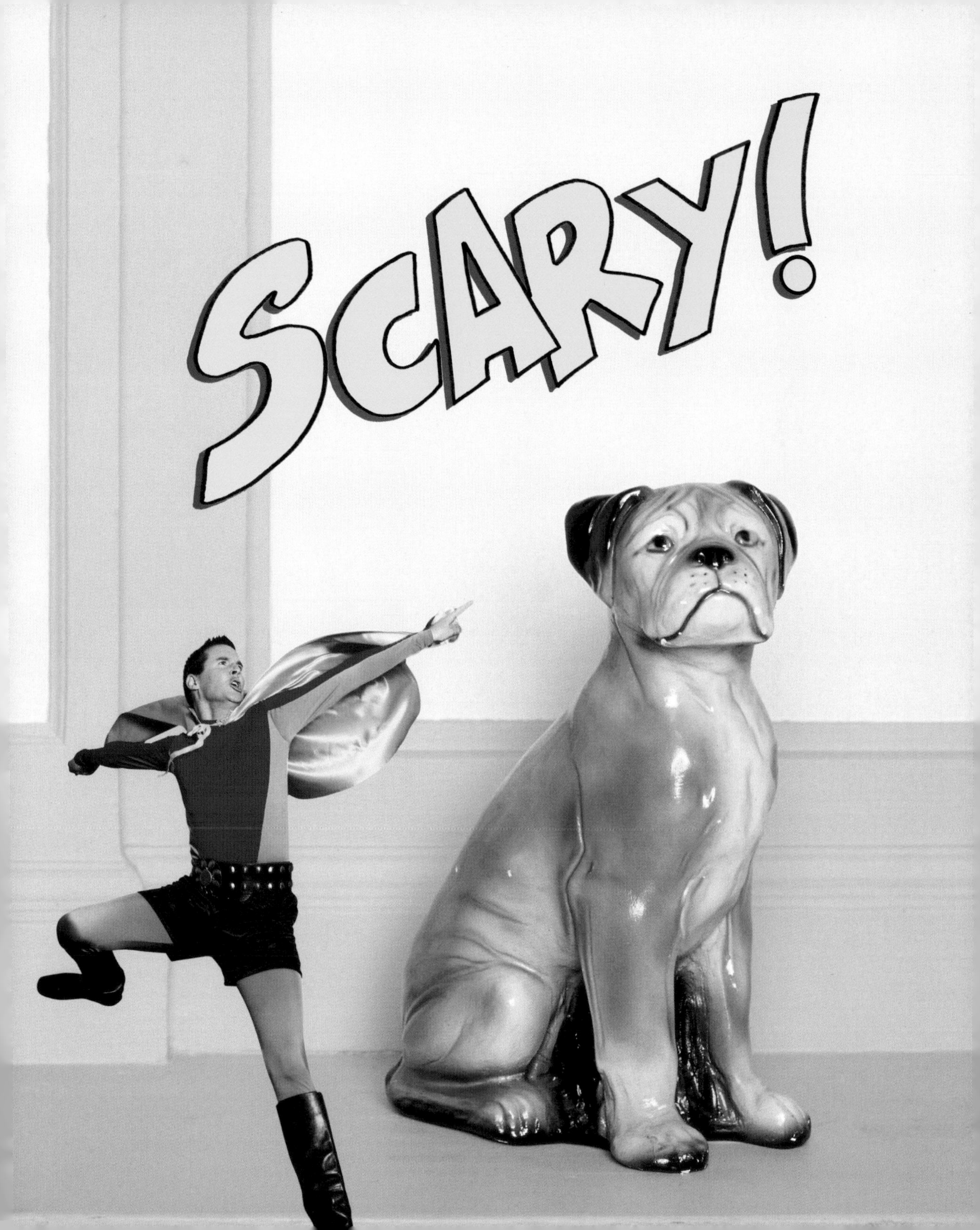
SCARY!

4 Disastrous Dining Rooms

So, anyway, onwards; let's meander further. But hold on a tick. Just what is this mysterious room? A study? A child's bedroom? A general dumping ground? But wait, isn't that a table lurking underneath all those old boxes and newspapers? No, it couldn't be. Surely. But yes – it is. Oh my God . . . it's the dining room . . .

Staying in is the new going out – and that's official. We don't know about you lot (actually we do 'cos we're in your homes every day), but we love nothing better than having our pals round for supper and gassing into the wee small hours, as the bubbly flows, the oysters are necked and the conversation turns to hard, fast gossip. In fact, our candle-lit soirées are famous! And sufficiently hedonistic to make Fielding's Tom Jones feel as equally at home as his modern-day namesake. To this end we SO take advantage of our own dining room, and can't understand why others don't do the same.

'CANDLESTICKS OF SATAN!! Literally!! The devil donated his feet for these extraordinary objects. Be afraid. Be VERY afraid.'

But hold it – you're thinking that most British homes don't HAVE a dining room, aren't you? Well, you'd be wrong. The nation, we can assure you, is covered in three-bed semis which have:

a) a 'through lounge diner'
b) a separate dining room, or
c) a space where a dining table could be easily positioned.

So that's how it should be. How it is, however, is a different kettle of dining fish altogether. As we crisscross Britain on our mission of interior enhancement, we see zillions of dining rooms that are either horribly under-utilised or overflowing with the wrong type of furniture. The space is there, but function and order are not.

In essence, all you need to create the perfect dining space is a room or zone that's large enough to accommodate a table and chairs. A little unity is useful when putting the visuals together (matching furniture is always a winner), but after that it should, technically, be easy to assemble a winning formula. Why is it, then, that we have to show you these dining disasters, instead of a raft of gorgeous rooms? Well, aside from the fact we'd be out of a job if Great Britain was decoratively present and correct . . . we actually rather relish the bad taste. Funny that, huh?

HEMEL HEMPSTEAD BEFORE – The relationship between tables and chairs is always crucial in any well-planned dining room. Clearly there's a trial separation going on here! It's a tragic fact but this dining room is representative of so many in Britain today.

HEMEL HEMPSTEAD AFTER – Totally under-utilised when we arrived, this dining room needed a good kick in the ass, a major clear out, a full paint job and some budget furniture to bring it bang up to date. You've got to question why the owners couldn't be bothered when it had all this potential . . .

EDINBURGH BEFORE – Take one perfectly grand Scottish room. Fill it with the contents of your garage and – hey presto! – you've got somewhere with all the decorative panache of a prison waiting room. Anyway, must dash – visiting time over. Thank God.

EDINBURGH AFTER – Mixing a chunky table and chairs with modern wallpaper and lighting creates a cool contemporary feel. And it's fair to say that the room is a wee bit nicer than before, huh?

MANCHESTER BEFORE – Aye, it's like a scene from *Abigail's Party*. A stage set of suburban seventies design, this cocktail of bad taste left us shaken and VERY stirred.

'It's like a Spanish taverna on acid. But I just can't fathom that carpet...'

MANCHESTER AFTER – It's certainly FAR hipper to be square and
that's why we made sure the arch went out with our ark. Note the carpet –
the black and white horrid florid fiasco has gone. Okay, so the new one's
plain ... but much less of a pain.

FOLKESTONE BEFORE – Dining chairs? Check. Crockery? Albeit on the wall, but Check. Telescope? (*Telescope?*) Check. And dining TABLE? Hmm. CHECKED OUT.

FOLKESTONE AFTER – We know it looks fab but it was really easy, honest! So what was our secret? Well, we simply had that Greek wedding and smashed the plates. And then we stole some furniture from the reception and made a dining room.

So what makes a good dining room?

Well, colour, for a start. Throughout the ages, popular
dining-room colours have changed beyond recognition.
Back in Victorian times, tastes were entirely different
and colour scheming tended to be WAY more dramatic.
Victorians believed red to be the perfect shade to
promote conversation (and digestion) and their dining
rooms were often deep claret or strong burgundy.
But then again their rooms tended to err on the grand
side. And size truly does matter – if your space is more
restricted, you have to be canny with your choice
of palette, or guests will be utterly overwhelmed.

These days we consider it good sense to keep schemes
predominantly neutral, and to add colour via strong
accessories that can be changed as moods dictate,
or via an accent wall to introduce a little drama.

Colin McAllister, shaken, not stirred.

J and C's Top Ten Dining Room No Nos

1 Overpowering colour schemes – mood should be low key to ensure your guests don't faint. Or vomit.

2 Small rooms crammed with furniture – if space is limited don't stuff in loads of extra chairs. Throw two smaller soirées instead of one where everybody is elbow to elbow. And the real bonus? You get to drink twice as much champagne. Vintage, of course. NEVER domestic.

3 Don't overpower lighting – side lighting or lots of flickering candles will add much more mood than a hundred-watt bulb could ever hope to.

4 Don't dual-purpose – a computer or workstation in the corner of your dining room will only distract your diners. When guests are due, hide all your technology in a cupboard. Give them a night off work, for heaven's sake …

5 Distance is everything – where possible select a room for dining that is near the kitchen and far from the toilet.

6 Lack of music – remember the ears! Gentle background is best in most situations to allow conversation to flow …

7 Wobbly chairs – nothing worse for your guests than the ominous feeling they're about to bust their ass! Get the screwdriver out and tighten them up. The chairs, that is …

8 Uneven tables – you know how annoying it is in a restaurant when you have to ask the waiter to pop a folded napkin below one of your table legs to balance you up. Save your guests that inconvenience by sanding longer legs to size. Or supply individual stacked sandals to balance things up.

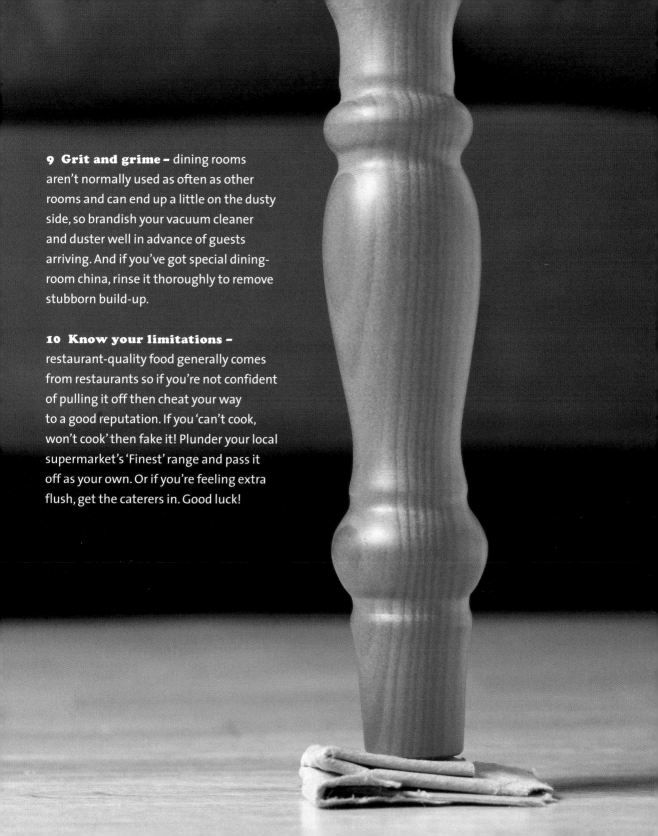

9 Grit and grime – dining rooms aren't normally used as often as other rooms and can end up a little on the dusty side, so brandish your vacuum cleaner and duster well in advance of guests arriving. And if you've got special dining-room china, rinse it thoroughly to remove stubborn build-up.

10 Know your limitations – restaurant-quality food generally comes from restaurants so if you're not confident of pulling it off then cheat your way to a good reputation. If you 'can't cook, won't cook' then fake it! Plunder your local supermarket's 'Finest' range and pass it off as your own. Or if you're feeling extra flush, get the caterers in. Good luck!

5 Catastrophic Kitchens

Colin and Justin, moments after being asked
to wash up three teaspoons and a mug.

So, that's the dining room sorted. But if you're going to start hosting all these fabulous dinner parties, we'd best find the kitchen. Ready? Are you sure . . . ?

Ah yes, the kitchen: the heart of the home. That crucial make or break area when you're selling, and, more importantly, the place where the family comes together to share quality time. Kitchens should be temples of cleanliness and creativity. They should be smart, efficient spaces but also warm and welcoming. All in all, they are hugely important, so why are thousands of them in a despicable and desperate mess? It's enough to give you indigestion.

Let's take a look at one absolutely typical British kitchen. And prepare yourself, dear readers, this one's depressing . . .

WHEN GOOD HOMES GO BAD #6
KITCHEN-SINK DRAMA!

Look at the zillion things going on in here. Knick-knacks, fridge magnets, patterned curtains, café nets, floral borders, surface clutter, wall plaques. Not to mention the fruit-tree stencil behind the cooker. Mmmm. Lovely.

Ask yourself this question: do I feel energised and ready to create a Delia Smith soufflé in here, or am I about to fill the air with expletives in the style of Gordon Ramsay? If you ask us, the answer is 'f**k, b****cks, b****rd …'

'Yes, it's the same kitchen, but without the skip load of junk and that ginormous British Racing Green fridge freezer. Thank the lord for integrated appliances.'

Winner or Sinner?

So, do you have a catastrophic kitchen? If any of the following apply to YOU, then your culinary space could indeed be more *puker* than pukka:

 You can't cook what you want when you want.

 Preparing a simple meal is so stressful you'd rather eat out.

 You only have a foot and a half of workspace to do all of your chopping, slicing and dicing. But you're lucky. You still have ten fingers ...

 Your kitchen doesn't provide enough space for guests and certainly can't accommodate more than one cook at a time.

 You're totally overrun with gadgets.

 Your floor, surfaces and doors are sticky. In fact, your entire kitchen is held together with chip fat and dog hairs.

 Your appliances are squeezed together like a scratch and dent electrical store.

 If you hesitated for even a moment over any point, then don't delay; it's time for some SERIOUS kitchen action. But, hey, if you think YOUR kitchen is dire, take a look over the page ...

Colin and Justin: Giving
bad taste the cold shoulder.

WHEN GOOD HOMES GO BAD #7

1970S STRIPES

Talk about Hell's Kitchen...

Okay, so some kitchens look like the temple of a domestic goddess and others look like a 1970s stripy sweater waiting for a Pulp revival. While beige and brown stripes may look the part on a grungy rock star (yes, we're talking Javis again), in a kitchen? Forget it.

Can you spot the dodgy extra feature in this kitchen? Here are a few clues. It's not a chicken rotisserie function, or an eye-level microwave, or a built-in cappuccino maker. No, it's a toilet! EEUUGH! Yes, look carefully and you'll spot THE DOWNSTAIRS BOG peeking out from the old larder in the centre of the room. Just next to the kitchen sink. Nice. Just imagine it – granddad on the throne and dinner for a party of six. Now that's what we call open-plan entertaining.

So, can you spot the six kitchen catastrophes in this room?

1 More grease on the hob than on John Travolta.

2 Dirty, dated brown stripy units.

3 LOVELY 1970s Jurassic leaf print tiling.

4 Terrible layout.

5 Ill-fitted appliances – white goods strewn across the room like a kitchen discount warehouse.

6 And that pièce de résistance – a toilet!

Now let's look at how this kitchen should be ...

Is that chair near the sink for the toilet queue?

Fab touch – we're loving the hanging bin bag right next to the cooker. Though judging by the state of that hob, that's the first place any food made in here is going . . .

The fruits of our labour – a spectacular family dining/kitchen.

First things first. The toilet is gone (funnily enough), relocated to a cupboard under the stairs. Hoorah! So it's goodbye to peeing and pooing … and hello to ahhing and oohing! The rest of the space now positively encourages cooking, dining and sharing. And we didn't stop there …

Quality of rooms is more important than quantity, so we knocked the dining room and the kitchen into one generous family-orientated space. Lush.

'Stainless' steel has a horrible habit of being less than stainless, so on this occasion, as there were so many children in the house, we opted for stainless steel lookalike doors that still have all the appeal of the real thing but without those annoying fingerprints.

Using the same flooring between two adjoining areas dramatically increases the feeling of space.

To simplify the design of your kitchen, make sure that appliances are hidden, or at least colour-coded to fit in with your choice of doors.

One way to make a kitchen appear larger and fresher is to remove unnecessary items from the work surface. You've got cupboards, after all, so why not use them?

Kneel down and give thanks: this room is now fit for a domestic goddess!

Grime is a Crime

We swear by that old saying: 'Where there's muck, there's ...
YUCK!!' Even if you do nothing else to update your kitchen,
it's absolutely crucial that you keep it clean.

So what causes kitchen gunge? Well, quite simply, the fact
that you can't be bothered to give everything a jolly good scrub.
And the worst offender? The deep-fat fryer. Health-busting fried
foods account for more grease and smells in British kitchens than
you could ever imagine. So either scrub and polish regularly ...
or ditch the fries, grease ball!

Even your uncooked foodstuffs can add to the problem. If you
don't rotate what's in your cupboards, you'll end up with dated
supplies lurking at the back, which will attract all manner of fungi,
beetles and bugs. There's nothing worse than chomping down
on a Gypsy Cream, only to discover its sell by is well by. And when
you do eventually throw the soggy biccies in the trash can, make
sure that your swing bin swings. Yup, don't wait until it's fit to
burst with sticky foodstuffs before you empty it out. A bin should
be clean as a pin, not stagnant with sin!

Key Kitchen Areas in the Fight Against Grime:

Window blinds.

Extractor hoods.

Ovens.

Gaps between appliances and units.

Cupboard floors and drawers.

Floors.

Fridge doors, seals and drains.

Bins.

In other words: EVERYWHERE! So snap on those rubber gloves, don your pinny and GET SCRUBBING!

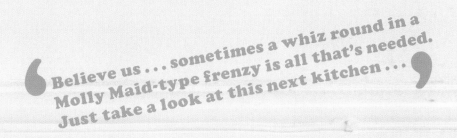

'Believe us . . . sometimes a whiz round in a Molly Maid-type frenzy is all that's needed. Just take a look at this next kitchen . . .'

'Just how are you meant to open that washing-machine door? And as for that exposed pipework . . . No wonder there's a first aid box under the sink – this is a design emergency!!'

'Luckily, our superpowers saved the day once more. After we'd quickly rejigged the existing units and given the whole place a crazy clean, it felt like a brand-new kitchen. Hell's bells: even the washing hung itself out to dry!'

Stop the press - call the kitchen cops!

Quick! Phone Max Clifford; we've got a tabloid headline –
'HAMILTONS IN DIRTY TRICKS SCANDAL'. Oh dear. Take a look
at the tragic kitchen of Neil and Christine Hamilton. Yup, those
terrible twins of evil certainly know how to put a chaotic kitchen
together. Let's take them to the courtroom and accuse them of
despicable crimes against design and see if they plead guilty:

 Not enough storage, too much clutter
Clear out the crap and clean up your act. Surfaces – YES. Clutter – NO.

 Swollen units
Take some split particleboard doors, add water and watch your cupboards
turn into Weetabix.

 Carpet tiles
Squares from Sodom, these absorbent 12 x 12s soak up more dirt than
a tabloid newspaper.

 Pin boards
The enemy of the civilised world and simply a way of taking
clutter off worktops … and making it climb the walls.

'This conservative kitchen failed to win our vote.'

So, what was the verdict? Guilty, M'lud, of crimes against design! Throw the *How Not To Decorate* book at 'em. Now let's see how their kitchen should look:

The sentence delivered: 'Hard labour', as one wall comes down to reveal a sensible open-plan space for dining as well as cooking.

Kitchen Accessories from Hell

A great accessory can make a room. A terrible one can break it. If you've got any of these – GET RID. If you've got several of these – KEEP TAKING THE TABLETS.

Novelty egg cups – oh, the hilarity of seeing your breakfast vessel turn into a bald man.

Harvester-style toasters, kettles etc. – if your kettle is decorated with wheat sheaves, you have a problem. If you've got a matching toaster, mug tree, mugs, tea towels, kitchen roll holder . . . you need to sit down on your shell-backed sofa and seriously re-evaluate your life.

Curtains – absorbent banners of fabric, guaranteed to soak up all your cooking leaks and smells. Imagine a hanging sponge of gunge . . .

Picture placemats – a 'chocolate box' execution of a gypsy caravan? A dramatic fox-hunting scene? No No No No No. And No again . . .

3D fruit and veg tiling – yeah, let's stud the kitchen walls with apples and plums. Then again . . . LET'S NOT.

Holiday souvenirs – say no to memo boards, thermometers or egg timers marked 'A present from Morecambe/Blackpool/ Southport/Hell' . . .

Fridge magnets – who really needs messages fastened to their chiller? It's a fridge, after all, not a bleedin' flipchart.

Ornaments – kitchens should be precise and functional, not used as a showcase for your collection of 'genuine bone china' birds. Do yourself a favour and buy that hammer . . .

Empty wine bottles arranged above your cabinets – what are you, a student? Recycle the glass collection and do your home – and the planet – a favour.

Mug trees – stack those cups high, dear. You'd have to be a mug to use one.

Spice racks – dusty, sticky and always filled with out-of-date spices that no one uses like oregano, fennel, ginger, scary, baby, sporty, posh . . .

Carrier bag collection – quick, call *The Guinness Book of Records*; we've just broken the world record for the most plastic bags in one drawer.

WHEN GOOD HOMES GO BAD #8
FROM GRIMER TO DINER . . .

Before

This homeowner just didn't seem to care. Not only was her kitchen badly in need of a right good scrub, it had all the personality of a professional darts player.

Our hit list

Permafrost freezer

Please introduce the word 'defrost' to this owner's vocabulary. Scott of the Antarctic is still lost somewhere in the back of that freezer.

Lack of everything

No surfaces, no cupboards, no reason . . .

Surface pipework

Looking like the *Titanic*'s engine room.

Smashed washing-machine door

That must have been some boil wash!

Cat beds on top of fridge

We love pussy, but NOT on top of the fridge.

Rubber gloves and broom

Must be art installations. They've certainly never been used.

Quick Quiz: Q. How many magnets can one fridge take?
A. Judging from these pictures: 9473.

After

A stylish place for everything with everything in its place –
this streamlined haven is slickly inspired by those fabby
1950s American diners. Check out all the steel, the candy
colouring and the signature chequer floor. Notice how we
use the word 'inspired' – nope, this ain't a theme park of
Elvis pictures and Stars and Stripes; more a modern design
that will appeal to a young homeowner. Leave the idea
of theming firmly in the past …

Kitchen Units

Traditionally, American 'diner'-style kitchens were in fun candy colours such as hot pink or baby blue but, rather than be too literal and risk creating a kitchen that would quickly date, we installed a white kitchen and added colour via other sources. This way it's easier to amend the look in future, as plain white kitchens can be the basis for a variety of styles.

Pipework

Sure, it's cheaper to 'surface mount' when installing central heating pipes, but do you really want your home to look like the *QE2*'s boiler room? This kitchen was horribly scarred across the ceiling and behind the boiler but, rather than rip it all out and start again, we asked a chippie to create a suspended ceiling to cover the problem. And good news! Doing this also provided a gap into which we could neatly install recessed lighting. Find a fault, make a feature, say we!

Steel Appeal

We used loads of stainless steel finishes to provide uniformity and to add an ultra-modern touch in this room. Steel looks clean and precise, and if it's kept clean (which can be a devil of a job) it will reflect light, to ensure your kitchen sparkles and shines by day or night.

In the Pink

The colour in this room comes largely from two sources – the hot pink Smeg fridge and the pink glass splash-back, both of which add a gorgeous quality edge to our design.

Your Name in Lights!

To create a funky personalised US diner light feature, we contacted a signage company and asked them to create a neon sign (using our homeowner's name) in candy pink. As with all electrics, make sure you leave installation to the professionals. And keep well away from water!

Flooring

We achieved the black and white chequerboard effect by using a tough, cushioned vinyl flooring. When it comes to laying such a product, make sure your floor is completely smooth and free of grit, which could show through some of the cheaper products on the market. And remember that laying this kind of material is a job best left to the experts. Home-laid lino, in our experience, always fits badly and shows up all sorts of irregularities. Remember our motto – 'If you buy cheap, you buy twice . . .'

Cupboard Love

Many of us – sorry, many of you – appear to enjoy cluttering up kitchen work surfaces with packets of cereal, old coffee makers and other ghastly gadgets and knick knacks. Are your counter tops for working or for storing? In a nutshell, cupboards are for storing and worktops are for working. So get rid of all your unused paraphernalia . . . even if that means taking it back to the car boot sale where you bought it in the first place. Or pop it in a municipal dump and put it out of its misery.

Environmental Alert

Organised, legal dumping does NOT constitute a waste of resources. All you're doing is simply recycling space – which is worth much, much more . . . And it's not like you'll be replacing it with more stuff, is it? Hmm?

Inspect Your Gadgets!
The eight big offenders...

1 Yoghurt makers – do you really eat enough of this to justify the loss of space and the initial expense? Strictly for thrush sufferers only...

2 Bread makers – believe us: if you use yours more than once, you're doing well. Bread makers are big and bulky so why not simply buy a good quality loaf and heat it gently in the oven?

3 Filter coffee maker – fill the jug with water, get the coffee, get a filter paper, pour the water in, wait till it boils, wait for coffee to drip. Forget it – make yourself a Nescafé instead. Or go to Starbucks...

4 Soda Streams – do you really like adding gas to your own flat juice? And if you've got one, when was the last time you used it? Truth?

5 Ice cream maker – what? With our climate?

6 Wine cooler – erm, don't you have a fridge?

7 Fat-free grills – get over them and dry-fry or oven-bake instead.

8 Toastie makers – what a load of hassle! Make yourself a sarnie instead, and save the roof of your mouth a thousand scorchings while you're at it.

WHEN GOOD HOMES GO BAD #9

TRAGIC MAGIC

Before

Welcome to Harry Potter and the kitchen from hell. Just look at this moon-and-stars decorated kitchen. Magic? Well, maybe, but then so too was the Wicked Witch of the West. And look what happened to her. Were the family responsible for this travesty being serious when they decorated with a magical theme, or was it all just a wizard wheeze? Hmm? The end result, as far as we're concerned, is more tragic than magic, what with its star-spangled kickboard, star-spotted ceiling and matching blind. Yup, someone is definitely a design dunce at Hogwarts. It's time to wave our designer wands and make it all disappear …

Our Hit List

Star-painted textured ceiling
The homeowners love stars … but this one's more a disa-star.

Paint-effect doors
Like claws dragged across a prison wall. Dreadful. And those ridiculous moon-and-stars kickboards and the 'luxurious' gold-painted handles make the whole thing ten times worse.

Micro storage
Why do homeowners allow their microwaves to become a gathering point for all sorts of clutter?

Lack of cooker splash-back
All those cooking spills could ruin the 'wonderful' effect on the wall.

 Tile-effect lino

Mmm, that blue, mouldy toast look is so NOW. Well, at least those ripped and peeling bits provide a fab place for even more dirt and grime to lurk.

 Wiring

Meanwhile, we are LOVING the miles of cable handily stashed behind the missing kickboard. When stretched across the kitchen to a plug socket it not only allows the owner to power the washing machine but also creates a handy washing line!

After

Blimey – get a load of this. Have we transported you to the set of *Sex and the City*? Is this a modern, iconic take on practical minimalism or what? And is this one of the simplest yet most stylish kitchen makeovers EVER? Why, yes, yes and yes again! And, guys – it's NOT brain surgery! It's just a simple redesign, one that balances colour and accommodation. And we're proud as punch! Who said the humble British semi can't enjoy a bit of sexy Manhattan chic?

Kitchen Unit Colour

And you thought pic 'n' mix was something you chomped at the cinema. Here, we mixed three complementary door colours (in the same style) to create our own contemporary take on glamour. And get this – mixing didn't cost any more cash as each door came from the same budget price range. So don't just stick to what the catalogue says – let your imagination go wild.

Free Up Space

If you're stuck for space then integrate appliances into wall cupboards as well as base units. Sure, we popped in a hidden dishwasher and washing machine at base level – as you might expect – but we also positioned the microwave at eye level to a) make it easier to use, b) free up workspace, and c) add to the eye-candy factor.

Flooring

We used white tiles on the floor to lighten up the space and found that their regular pattern really added to the overall sharp, sexy feel. If you're worried that ceramic tiles might be too cold underfoot then worry no more – we added underfloor heating, which doesn't cost as much as you might think. Expect to pay from £300.

Lighting

When you're planning your kitchen don't forget proper lighting. Here, an overhead spread of spotlights illuminates the entire room, while task lighting – under eye level – lights up the work zone perfectly.

Visible Spending

When spending on your kitchen, it's worth splashing out on a few very visible items – especially if you want to create a Wow! factor. A 'GLAM' (Gorgeous, Lifestyle Accessory Must-have) like this Smeg fridge, for example, provides heaps of appeal in this modern space.

So, are you getting the hang of this yet? Are you ready to trade decorative home trauma for sheer designer perfection? We've touched on several rooms already, proffering C and J tips as we go, but we think it's time to open another door …

'Say your prayers, we're going up the stairs …'

6 Bloody Awful Bedrooms

Bedrooms. Temples of peace and tranquillity, where the soul finds succour and the heart is warmed. Gorgeous, well-planned nests where you re-energise after the woes of busy days and frantic weeks. That's certainly how they should be. And yet most British bedrooms are the visual equivalent of someone running a cheese grater over your chin. It's a tragedy of *Hamlet* proportions. Delve into this chapter and witness patterns that clash like dustbin lids cartwheeling down the street in the middle of the night. Visually noisy, to say the very least. And, of course, downright ugly.

Considering that most of you lazy loafers spend somewhere between a third and a quarter of your lives holed up in the sack, we find it astonishing that you treat your bedrooms with such disrespect. Come on – this is where you rest your weary head at night, but it's also where you get to play out your biggest fantasies. Well, we won't go there, thanks very much, but whatever you're up to in the boudoir, for Gawd's sake GIVE YOURSELF A DECENT BACKDROP.

THERE'S NO REST FOR THE WICKED

What is it about you lot and bedrooms? Why do you make life so hard, when it could be oh so easy? Creating an indulgent bedroom isn't exactly taxing – anyone with a modicum of style can pull it off. If you're in any doubt simply opt for a neutral scheme and add colour and style notes via bedding and curtains. That way you'll have no reason to get it wrong ... unless, of course, you just can't be arsed.

Trident tested ... You don't have to fork out all that much to create the perfect room for love ... and snoring.

Feather bed, anyone? Justin offers himself up for a good plucking.

In our design travels we've had to endure the nightmare of a billion bloody awful bedrooms. And quite frankly, we don't see why you should get away with it. Over the next few pages we're going to guide you through the bedrooms of Britain. And before that gets your pulse racing, we should make it clear these are some of the least sexy places on Earth. A roundabout in Slough has more erotic potential.

Aye, these rooms are so bad you'll be waking up in a cold sweat for weeks to come. But darlings, we promise – it will all be worth it when you transform your own bedroom into a boudoir of bliss. Don't thank us all at once ...

A LESSON IN BEDROOM BEDLAM IN FOUR EASY STAGES

If it's that easy to set the style stakes, why does this bedroom look as if it's been lying at the bottom of a river for the last couple of years? LAZINESS, that's why. There's simply no excuse for letting your most private inner sanctum collapse into such a godawful state. And the main offenders? The whole bloody lot. Note the easyJet-orange colour scheme and hold on to your lunch as you take in the horror of that GREASY headboard. Or those 3D stick-on butterflies. But it doesn't stop there. Let's talk about that demonic, diagonal-design, prison-issue quilt cover. And how about that yellow and moss-green bedroom furniture? WHY? WHY? WHY? Oh, and note the wall-mounted TV – perfectly positioned to take your eye out as you enter the room. Nice. Aye – 'tis a grim scene but it's one that's alarmingly familiar. Now let us tell you the MOST shocking bit. This is the bedroom of an adult couple. You heard right . . . it's NOT a kid's room.

Lesson 1

'For the love of God . . . check that greasy headboard! It looks like it's had chip fat poured over it . . .'

So how did we make the room mature? Well, the simple solution was to tone it all DOWN … by livening it all UP. The owners – a perfectly lovely couple who, by their own admission, were 'just a bit mental' – desperately wanted to inhabit a brightly hued world. But, whenever they spun the colour wheel, they screwed up. We (to their initial horror) painted everything white as they looked on. Then we went a bit nuts – but only because we knew we could get away with it – and added an accent wall of black and themed everything else bright red. We're not going to describe how we went about it in any more detail because you can see the transformation for yourselves.

Thank GOD we got there in time. Otherwise our guilty owners might have lost the decorating battle of good versus evil. That greasy headboard could have sprouted teeth and eaten them … and just think of the mess *that* would have made. Actually, it probably wouldn't have looked any worse.

But the horror story continues. If you thought that bedroom was bad, allow us to unfold yet another gem from the *How Not To Decorate* vault. Cast your eyes, if you will, over our next piece of damning visual evidence.

'Dorothy emerged from the tornado, ruby shoes intact, wondering if Toto had also survived . . .'

Lesson 2

When we saw this room for the first time, we had no idea what was going on. Had there been a break-in? Had the owners had some type of domestic drama, which had resulted in the whole room being smashed to smithereens? Well, actually, no. This room has in fact been destroyed by that natural disaster known as CHILDREN. Our homeowners were a perfectly nice couple who between them had a staggering SEVEN kids. And ONE three-bed semi in deepest Letchworth.

In defence of the parents we have to say . . . actually, there can be NO defence. So let's look at the evidence. For starters, there's nothing like a bit of privacy, is there? With that in mind, note the curtains. Or, rather, the lack of them. The clothes obviously couldn't stand another second in those collapsing cupboards and made a suicidal leap on to the floor. The vacuum cleaner might have made an attempt to hoover up some of the debris but clearly it had lost the will to suck and, probably, to live. RIP.

(And remember: this is the home of REAL people. Perfectly normal real people, with perfectly lovely children, who, thank God, were still young

enough to escape the damaging effects of living in a jumble sale.)
We couldn't even think straight in there (no comment!) but after we'd
downed half a bottle of whisky to settle our nerves we found it simple
enough to create a sense of order.

Balancing 80 per cent industrial cleaning with a modest 20 per cent
design we set to work immediately. We painted pink, vibrant red and
pale blue stripes along all the walls and pulled the look together with
bedding in similar tones. And the cost of this, ahem, massive makeover?
£80 for the bedding, cushions and throws for all three beds (do the
supermarket sweep, darlings, and pick up entire duvet sets for less than
a tenner a pop), £120 for carpet and £45 for paint. Aye – less than £250
all in. And if it's all in, why wrestle! We harvested the beds from around
the house and brought them up to date by sanding off the orange varnish
and rubbing the open grain with a little lime wax. Which cost £4.99 a tin.
Oh my God, we're good . . .

Lesson 3

Surely no one ever had sex here – at least not with another person. Can't you just imagine the woman who put this look together, sitting at her drawing board in a pair of gumboots and a hair net, Horlicks dribbling down her winceyette nightie? She's flicking the pages of *People's Friend* with a single vision: to make the spare bedroom as barren as is humanly possible. 'That'll keep the house guests at bay!' she grins as she plumps for the most unflattering overhead lighting she can find. 'And if I confuse people further by popping in a wall of kitchen units, nobody will ever come back. I'll save a fortune in hospitality!'

'The only good thing about this room? It took us three seconds to clear it all into a skip.'

By Jove. It's a corker. It used to look like a downmarket B&B in some dodgy seaside town; aye, £15 a night, and even that would be a rip-off. Now with a wee touch of the Orient, it recalls the kind of luxury you'd find in an East Meets West boutique hotel.

The secret was to strip everything out and work our way back up from a new cream carpet. While it all looks like the height of luxury, we were careful to select new furniture without breaking the bank. The entire kit came from the high street and even the exotic looking bedding and cushions came from humble sources such as catalogue return shops and salvage stores. Believe us – we didn't overspend on this occasion. The magic is in the vision – which doesn't cost a penny – and in the final styling.

So what did we do? Well, the desperate collapsing louvre doors couldn't be saved so we ripped them out and replaced them with inexpensive carpenter-made pine frames which we filled with fretwork boards (the kind of product that's designed to be made into radiator cabinets) and then stained everything darkest oak to match the four-poster bed. Believe it or not we spent a grand total of just £650 on this room. And that small price included paint, carpets and furniture as well as cushions, throws and artworks. Is it any wonder our homeowner wept as we showed her the end result? Saying that, dry-eyed homeowners are not a problem on our shows: we always carry an emergency spray-bottle of glycerine to prompt those stubborn tears.

'I'm mortified that this is a Scottish house. This horror story is by the hands of our own kin...'

We never did find out what happened to the bed. Perhaps it just got fed up living on a carpet that looked so tired it was practically comatose. Or maybe it was stolen by the same people who nicked the wallpaper... straight off the wall. And we dread to think about the bedding that adorned it. A candlewick, perchance, in claret and gold? Or possibly a putridly patterned polyester joy that set off static sparks? Whatever happened to it, the bed was one less hellish thing for us to remove before we started our massive transformation.

We were particularly horrified by this one, as it's in our own homeland. Well, Edinburgh to be precise – forty-five miles east of Glasgow. Of course, you'd NEVER see this level of hell in Glasgow. Never...

It's the detailing we love – note, for instance, how the ugly radiator has been shoved directly across a perfectly lovely Victorian fireplace. FOR THE LOVE OF GOD: that's just wrong! It looks like a mouth with a gag on it. Another bugbear is that snap-together, built-in cabinetry over the bed. These are always virtually inaccessible and so wind up either empty or crammed full of stuff you never use. And who, after all, wants to sleep with a pile of discarded junk overhead? One shove during animated bed shenanigans and it'll fall off the wall and knock you out. Bit of a passion killer, huh? Hellish, horrid and tacky.

Hallelujah – your favourite fairy godfathers have been. Sure, it was
a monster job to repair the carnage but we got there. Like gutting a fish,
we cleared out every bit of bad taste and got back to a basic shell. Then
we started again. And take it from us: this room didn't just LOOK bad –
it WAS bad. To the very core. The rickety wall lamps had enough power
surging through their dangerously exposed cables to give Old Sparky
a run for its money, which meant we had to rewire the whole lot. And
as for the plasterwork . . . Well, the only thing holding that to the wall
was the woeful wallpaper. And as you know, most of that had already
fallen – or been ripped – off. We had to replaster and then skim the entire
room to give us a smooth surface upon which to imprint our new and
gorgeous look.

But there was one piece of good news. We found some common ground with the misguided owners. They told us that their favourite colour was red. Which, handily, is also one of ours. So it became our accent shade of choice and, contrasting it with purest white, we set to work.

But hold it just a minute. What the heck's that funny-looking padded platform in the middle of the room? The thing with the cushions on it? Oh, don't panic – that's just a little trick we employ from time to time to give our homeowners somewhere comfy to sleep. We call it a 'bed'. And doesn't it look just gorgeous with all those tonal textiles tying in perfectly with the accent wall of eastern crested wallpaper? (Wallpaper printed especially for us by Timorous Beasties, Scotland's leading manufacturer of quality wallcoverings.)

And, finally, our archaeological excavations behind the radiator revealed a truly beautiful hearth that now warms the room beautifully. Gag removed and cleaned out (we got a proper Mary Poppins-type chap with a HUGE pole to do the business), it's now a strong focal point that also provides a useful shelf for mirrors and accessories. Job done. Moving on . . .

Ten Bedroom No Nos

1 Mattresses on the floor – cool, low-slung living this ain't. Unless, of course, you're from the Orient and futons are your thing. Otherwise they're more student than stupendous so DON'T go there.

2 Candlesick, sorry candleWICK, bedspreads – even yer granny hates these now. So ditch 'em and choose a self-coloured duvet instead.

3 Messy computers and a Spaghetti Junction of cables cluttering up your dressing table – would you want to look at a PC when you're getting jiggy with it? On second thoughts ... DON'T answer that.

4 Dirty laundry – how difficult can it possibly be to run a tidy boudoir? When you pull your kecks off, stick 'em in the laundry basket. Don't leave them lying around for days on end like some crazy person.

5 Dirty sheets – bed linen should be changed every few days. Your body, believe it or not, expels up to a pint and a half of sweat every single night. Nice. You do the maths.

6 Poor illumination – bedtime reading material (easy!) should be clearly visible when you're propped up on your pillow. You'll go blind if you're not careful.

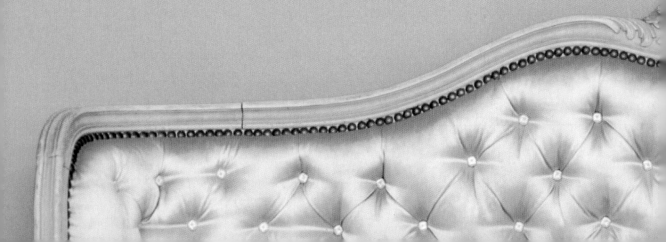

7 Sort it, stash it, store it – there's little worse than leaving rubbish and other 'stuff' hanging around your bedroom like a bad smell. If you don't use it or wear it any more, then give it to charity or pop it discreetly in the bin. And don't think that out of sight is out of mind – shoving everything under the bed is not the answer.

8 Overbearing wallpapers – remember our mantra; less is more. Keep bedroom wall coverings low key. Avoid enormous repeat-print papers which can overpower smaller spaces and choose smaller, more subtle patterns instead.

9 Avoid ceramic and stone floors – unless you happen to live in Tuscany or somewhere similarly warm and gorgeous. In Britain, your feet will be blocks of ice by the time you've made it to the loo in the middle of the night.

10 Don't let pongy odours ruin the mood – remember to titillate your beak as much as you do your eyes: getting the smell factor right in your boudoir will help keep the mood fresh and exciting. Choose gorgeous olfactory delights like Jo Malone or Molton Brown room scents and candles. Darlings, you're worth it.

. . . Take our advice and you'll soon be saying yes, yes, YES!!

WHEN GOOD HOMES GO BAD # 10

CELEBRITY SPECIAL: WE'RE DESIGNERS – GET US OUT OF HERE!

'Time's up on this dated disaster area.'

'Tony should be given the slipper for this boring bedroom.'

We've all seen those eye-poppingly excessive pop-star abodes with sunken baths and glitzy gold taps and beds in the shape of horses. But more shocking than all of that is the BORING celebrity home. Cue King of the Jungle, veteran DJ Monsieur Le Tony Blackburn. Cast your eyes, if you will, over this little lot. Can you comprehend the plainness of his 'look'? Well, it sure baffled us. Boring, boring and boring again. We'd anticipated a little drama or even some gorgeous antiques dotted around the place. What we found, however, was a bedroom that belonged in a two-star motel. We looked for the Gideon Bible and the tea-making facilities but it seemed they'd checked out some time before . . .

   The best bit, though, was that Tony and his lovely wife Debbie gave us free range to do exactly what we wanted to their singularly unattractive love nest. Which, as it happened, was exactly what we planned to do anyway. With no evident bedroom interior design skills whatsoever, they needed to be ridden over roughshod. They needed to be brought up to date

'Tony's now set to be King of the Bedroom, not just King of the Jungle. Grrrrr!'

as a matter of extreme and critical design urgency and we were delighted to accept the challenge.

First we sifted through their furniture to see if there was anything at all that we fancied reusing. There wasn't. So we gave the entire lot to charity and started over.

That is, except for our biggest problem: that massive wall of wardrobes, looking for all the world like a giant bank of wooden filing cabinets. We simply didn't have the time (or budget) to remove them, so we redesigned them with the most giant nip 'n' tuck imaginable. After taking them down and forming apertures in some (no, of course we didn't do it ourselves – our talented builders did that job. Darlings, we're the visionaries . . .) we sent them off to a spray finishers to be lacquered glossy black. Next, we positioned fabric sections behind the apertures and rehung the whole lot exactly where they'd been before. And while we were at it we added a couple of new doors – to hide the TV – and some discreet brass handles.

Because the room was so box-like and bereft of any architectural detailing or period features, we added our own 'history' by installing a dado rail which we painted black to match. We created an extra sense of style by wallpapering below the rail with a lightly patterned design, and good quality repro antique furniture sealed the deal.

We entitled our scheme 'Monochrome French Antique' and added our only accent colour via gold-framed family pictures. By positioning a massive Bateau Lit centre stage and flanking it on either side with Queen Anne-legged dressing tables, we gave the room purpose, depth and, damn it, loads of dripping deluxe style. Which is, in conclusion, a look that's tonnes more glamorous than its toffee-brown predecessor. Enjoy.

'It's like a haemorrhage in the Pink Panther's lower intestine...'

Some Bedroom Quick Fixes

'What's that above the bed?' we asked, with a degree of
trepidation. 'It's a dream catcher,' replied our homeowner,
hanging her head in shame. 'Looks more like a nightmare to us,'
we chastised, letting our eyes settle on the orange pine furniture.
And then on the navy-blue radiator. And then on the wallpaper
and border. And then, finally, upon the caterpillar-shaped cushion
that was crawling across the pillows. Time for a wake-up call ...

The only new piece of furniture we bought was the bed. Everything else was reused. We stripped and waxed the orange pine until it screamed for mercy. We tore down the vile velour curtains and replaced them with off-the-peg shutters. We recarpeted, stripped wallpaper and painted the entire room white. Then, for decorative punch, we added an accent of funky wallpaper above the bed. And then, just because we could, we added 2314 cushions. Aaah . . .

Even Barbie would feel sick in here . . .

Room diagnosis – Ugly. Tatty. Misguided. Note the
inspired use of a plastic bin as a bedside table. And how
on earth are you meant to light that fire with half a pine
warehouse stuck to the hearth? Oh, sorry – we didn't
realise; it's KINDLING.

Room remedy – sand the floorboards. Obliterate the offensive pink walls with soft green emulsion. Paint the pine. Get several sheep to lie flat and motionless on the floor. Job done. A weekend's work for years of enjoyment.

'This room is sick! Even the carpet's got varicose veins.'

We loved doing this room even though it was one of our simplest transformations ever. After stripping the wallpaper and repainting the room, the rest of the project was easy as designer pie. We added a double bed, some new carpet and matching blinds and bedding. The results speak for themselves . . .

This SO makes sense. The son who previously occupied this room had long since left home but his parents had never got round to reappraising the space. And we're not going to spoon-feed you with lavish descriptions – you can see what we've done. Clever storage and a fold-down bed into the bargain. That's all we're saying.

‘Darling, I used to be so far back in the closet I might as well have been in Narnia . . .’

'Thank God it's Bonfire Night next week. Those wardrobes will be SO fabulous doused with petrol...'

Dispose of pink carpet. Lay new carpet. Apply paint to walls. Hit Ikea for some new wardrobes and then make the bed. When it's this easy why do people still screw it all up?

'Lilac wine! No, sorry ... make that lilac WHINE. This is what happens when the people with the blandest taste in the world try to colour coordinate ...'

We had the bed made to our specifications and placed it on a cool timber floor. Then we dressed the entire room with a low-key neutral scheme. What could have been easier?

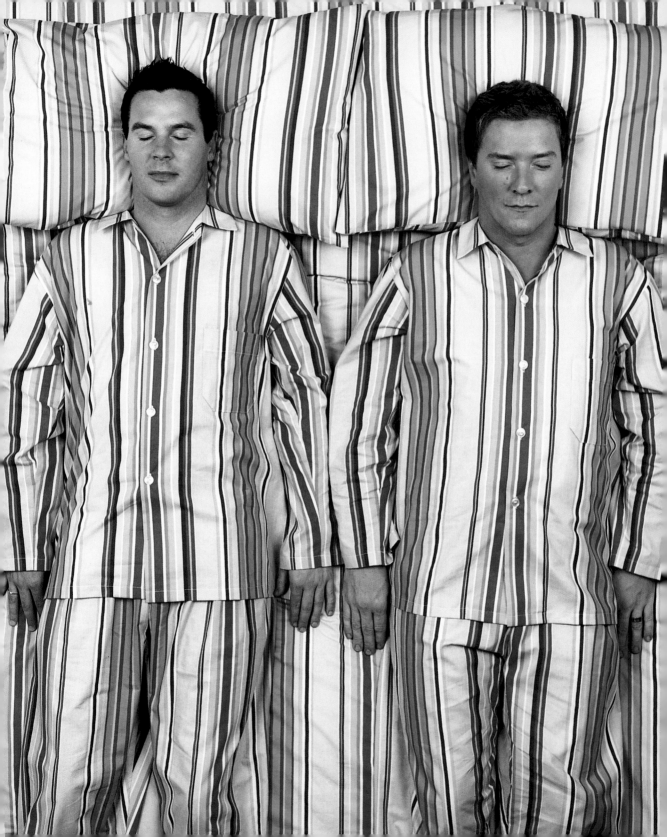

So, do you think you've got the message? Have all these pages of sublime bedrooms given you inspiration? Follow the examples we've given here and there'll be no more sleepless nights from now on …

After all that hard work, you probably want to lie down on your new, fabulous, self-coloured bed linens and dream of tasteful accent walls, mood lighting and tall, handsome Scottish designers … but wait. There's one thing you have to do after a hard day's designing. Yup – it's time for a nice relaxing soak, beacuse the bathroom is the last stop on our tour of travesties. Oh dear … something tells us this isn't going to be pretty …

7 Bilious Bathrooms

You've done it! You've made your way through a veritable house of horror, seen things no sane person should ever have to see ... Loos in the kitchen. Trolls in the living room. Justin in lycra. There's just one room to go, but boy – they may call it 'the smallest room', but there are some HUGE designer disasters going on here. Close your eyes, clip a peg on your nose, and prepare yourselves. It's time to enter: THE BATHROOM.

So, are you awash with success or simply a washout? What does your bathroom say about you? Well, judging by some of the ones we've seen, you're a right bunch of mingers who have absolutely no idea how to pick up a bar of soap ... let alone a paintbrush.

Now, we're not saying you have to invest in a wet room with all the trimmings. But it's easy to create a splash without breaking the bank. A good scrub, a simple white bathroom suite, a few neat and stylish accessories ... But we're getting ahead of ourselves. Darlings, you know the score by now: it's time for those scary 'before' shots ...

Christine Hamilton's poppy-filled bathroom was clearly created under the influence of opium . . .

Where better to start than with this bathing disaster. Aye – believe it or not this is how real life, ahem, 'celebrities' live. This is the bathroom of Neil and Christine Hamilton, the infamous pair who traded Parliament for panto. They actually did their ablutions (perish the thought) in this room. A room with a cracked timber toilet seat, a library of absorbent reading materials, a bathroom carpet (urgh! URGH!) and that most heinous of all bathroom design crimes – the paper-covered tiled wall. Bonkers as it sounds, Christine decided that the solution to perfectly acceptable plain white tiles was to wallpaper over the evidence! And no, we're not making it up – if you look closely you can clearly see the outline of the tiles beneath . . .

'Fancy a night on the tiles? Not in this Satanic bathroom, thank you very much. '

Just imagine: Christine at one end and Neil at the other, up to their nipples in Miss Matey. Torture . . .

'Oh, if only it was as easy to make over Neil and Christine . . .'

Thankfully, we were on hand to take this room from floral fiasco to cool, urban spa. And all it took was a new designer suite, some lovingly applied limestone tiling and some damn sexy timber finishes. Scented candles and subdued controllable lighting complete the picture.

A bathroom, after all, is a private place to cleanse, a soapy den of serenity and sanctuary. It is NOT somewhere to indulge your paint-fuelled, infantile fantasies via strings of dried seaweed and anchor-shaped mirrors. So cool it – DON'T swamp every surface with an ocean of pebbles, coral and dried puffer fish and DON'T stockpile back issues of *Heat* (much as we love it – it's our bible), *OK!* or *FHM*. Think about it: dried seaweed was once moist. If you place it in a room full of steam and water it'll become moist once again. Then it will rot. And do you really want the acrid smell of rotting kelp wafting through your home? Thought not. And as for pebbled surfaces; if your shelves and windowsills are swarming with stones, then where do you put all your toiletries, toothpastes and tampons? Try squeezing them in and you risk dropping a boulder down the loo every time you move. Lovely . . .

And why should you say no to lavatorial reading? Well it's a no-brainer – paper is absorbent and that's why you use it to, ahem, wipe your bottom. With this grizzly thought in mind, imagine your magazine pile as a giant sponge soaking up all the smells and liquid emissions from your WC. And let's not even think about the amount of germs that gather as reader after reader flicks through these tomes while, well, you can guess the rest . . . Who, after all, washes their hands before, during and after they read a magazine on the loo? Probably no one. Face it: it doesn't matter what your choice of reading material – it's all full of C**P!

Spot the mistake

Look at this picture for a moment and find the deliberate mistake. Sure, it's definitely a bathroom – you can tell that by the bath in the corner – but there's one notable omission. Can you see it? Sue your optician if you can't.

Other problems

 Lack of equipment. Loo roll holder, anyone? Bathroom cabinet? Mirror?

 Half-baked attempt at decor – oh, how the wrong choice of colour can completely kill a room.

 No bath panel – all that splashing around will ruin the exposed floorboards. And they'll quickly rot. Oh well, with no sink, no accessories and no taste, it was only a matter of time before there was no floor either.

(This family even had a *cat litter tray* tucked under their bath! Don't follow their example, unless you really *want* the pong of pussy pee and feline faeces wafting towards you as you're soaking in your tub ...)

Now let's look at how this bathroom should be ...

Can you spot the fundamental changes we've made? Aye, radical as it seems, this bathroom now has a SINK. Hoorah! And of course the redesigned space now functions much better as a family washroom and looks absolutely gorgeous into the bargain.

Points to Remember

 Bathroom suites should be white – coloured suites are as wrong as miniskirts on chunky thighs.

 Built-in mirrors help bounce light around to create a brighter, fresher space.

 Tiled surfaces are easy to clean and, because we've chosen a style that won't date, they'll look just as good in ten years' time. For God's sake don't get too fussy . . .

 Water-repellent Amtico flooring. Splish, splash, splosh, darlings, and the devil may care.

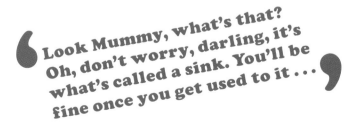
'Look Mummy, what's that? Oh, don't worry, darling, it's what's called a sink. You'll be fine once you get used to it . . .'

So. Just how bad is YOUR bog?

Stop flannelling and scrub your poor bathroom clean of these
dirty design disasters:

1 Toilet roll dolly – what can I do
with this spare loo roll? I know, I'll stick it
up Barbie's bottom and hope for the best.

2 Open-fronted medicine cabinets –
all your pills and potions on display?
Why not simply take out an ad in the
local paper and tell everyone how sick
you actually are?

3 Corner bath – this does NOT say
luxury … it simply says you don't have
enough space for a proper bath. To us they
reek of Brookside Close. And look where
that ended up. DOWN THE DRAIN. So,
if you've got a 90 degree lump of plastic –
ditch it and fit a proper bath instead.

4 Gold taps – STOP! Gold, after all,
rhymes with mould, old and scold. MOULD
– what your dated jewels are now covered
in. OLD – 'nuff said. And SCOLD – what
we'll do to you if you still have them after
reading this book.

5 Sea shell collection – no wonder the
shorelines of our great island are receding.
Shells, after all, belong on beaches not
in bathrooms.

6 Toilet brush – Satan's own wand
of woe, filled with faecal debris and God
knows what else. Avoid!

7 Terrible tiling – this includes sea-
life scenes, wheat sheaves and anything
with a vegetable pattern printed on to
it. Oh, and gold marble effect, smiley
faces, and Forever Friends ponies. You
get the gist …

8 Polystyrene ceiling tiles – vile,
vile and thrice vile. Great for scrunching
into dust to create fake snow for the kids'
nativity play but that's about it. They're
the devil's own homework so ditch them.

9 Carpets – hit or miss? Sh*t or p*ss,
more like. Carpets are fabric and fabrics
absorb liquid. Do we really need to spell
it out?

10 Mould – that fungal growth which
stretches along the rim of your bath,
across the tiles in your shower cubicle
and encrusts your ancient plastic shower
curtain … Arrrgh! Scrub it off with
bicarbonate of soda.

And a problem so bad that it stands outside our top ten. The coloured suite. NOOOOOOOOOOOOO... Come on; you know the rule – bathroom suites can be ANY colour ... as long as they're white.

We know we asked for a sea view but this is ridiculous . . .
there's something very fishy about this bathroom.

WHEN GOOD HOMES GO BAD # 11
THE AQUATIC BATHROOM

Bubbling Under

Let's get one thing straight – theming is NOT designing. Here's the proof: this bathroom was certainly inspired by the sea but the only thing it has in common with The Big Blue is that it makes us feel SEA SICK. Let's look at the evidence:

 Sea paint-effect tiles (like an aquatic dirty protest)

 Shell-studded walls (razor sharp and downright dangerous)

 Seaside-themed items everywhere – shell-encrusted towel rails, sailing boats, etc

 The ubiquitous seaside toilet seat

Blimey – it's time for the tide to turn ...

Bubbling Over

A bathroom should make you feel clean and refreshed BEFORE you've even turned on a tap … and that's precisely what this one does now. Hard to believe it's the same space, huh? Well, it is. Clean, crisp and precise, this smallest room is now smart and functional, yet still retains a definite identity. And yes, we've taken on board the owner's love of the sea, only this time with rather more subtlety.

Tiling

The use of larger rectangular tiles may seem at odds with the room's small proportions, but there's method in our designer madness. Using larger tiles, you see, limits the number of grout lines, thus 'de-fussing' the room and increasing the feeling of space. By using a navy-blue border tile, we added definition and provided a confident accent colour to use when buying towels and other accessories.

Position

Money-saving tip – when you're redoing your bathroom, try not to move things around too much. A plumber will charge much less for a 'one out/ one in' job than one that involves repositioning each item.

Indulge Yourself

It's official – home spas are *fabulous*. These days it's all about pampering, essential oils and, ahem ... keeping an eye on *Corrie*?? Well, your bathroom is your most personal space, so why not push the boat out and REALLY indulge yourself with a tub TV?

Equipment

Add simple luxuries like a shaver socket or an illuminated mirror to make life as easy as you can.

Steely Determination

It's easy to overlook but, to provide uniform style, make sure all your accessories match the colour of your taps. So that means no chrome faucets with gold accessories ...

'Two-tone ceramics and a Tilevision telly. What more could anyone ask for?'

LOOK OUT LADIES

Now, ladies, we don't want you getting into a lather. We're not being deliberately sexist but bathrooms do tend to be the domain of the female of the species. And therein lies another decidedly nasty design crime … the oestrogen-fuelled decorative overload known as 'girly overkill'.

So, what exactly is 'girly overkill'? Well, let us explain. It's when a bathroom becomes so feminine – and so anti-male – that it needs a placard of a little miss on the door. How many bathrooms have YOU seen that are festooned with frilly curtains, hanging beaded light cords or dust-covered Victorian dolls? And how many have you seen that are fit to burst with all manner of bath cubes, cuticle removers and hair-matted curlers? Blimey – we know it's hard work being a woman, but it's even harder on the poor blokes who have to share their bathrooms with the queens of clean!

Ban the Bog

Boys! Stand up for yourselves and ban these ladies things from your bog:

1 Anything overtly floral – do you really want to feel like you're tinkling in a forest?

2 Teddy bears/cute figurines – how old is your missus? Tell her to grow up.

3 Cuddly toys – as above. Only these are absorbent so even less suitable for a wet room.

4 Potpourri – okay, so it might smell like a synthetic alpine forest to start with . . . but within days it just smells of dust.

5 Scrunchies – hanging baskets of wet, dead skin. Nice.

6 Fourteen bottles of shampoo/conditioner/ body spray, etc., etc. – why so many? Just how dirty are you?

7 Personal items – out of sight, out of mind. Period.

BOYS BEWARE

Now admit it, fellas. You're not exactly the cleanest of toilet-goers
are you? You know what we mean – it's a frantic sprint, seat up, splash,
forget to flush and forget to wash hands. And before you know it you're
back in front of the telly with your zip down and a kebab in your hand.
Or else it's a veritable sit-down protest where you're in there for the night,
poring over the papers as you do some of your finest thinking and stinking!

So when is a bathroom too 'blokey'? Well, that's easy to explain.
If it's littered with unused Christmas gift sets (Hai Karate, Brut, Old Spice –
thanks Aunty Betty), has no loo roll (where do some boys wipe their
bottoms?) or if the shower curtain is more fungus than fabric, you're
well on the way to creating an exclusion zone for girls.

Men Behaving Badly

Now it's your turn, girls – liberate yourselves and insist your bloke gives these items the heave-ho:

1 Lads mags – well-thumbed, absorbent sheets of paper left next to the WC. For the love of God, they're 'LOADED' with all manner of dirty deposits.

2 Underpants – is that the face of Christ we can see in that discarded pair of Calvin's? No, it's just a horrid pair of pongy pants looking for a laundry basket.

3 Toenail clippings – put them in the bin or flush 'em down the loo. Just don't leave them there!

4 Short and curlies – nothing worse than a plughole that looks like a giant spider!

5 A dirty, dated dressing gown – either covered in last night's curry or some suspiciously currified rear fingerprints.

'Sexual equality: a very masculine sunken tub and matching Roman sink harmoniously exist with girly floral tiles and that tasteful gold swan tap. Yeah right! Granny's ashes are a nice optional extra . . .'

'Ahh, that's more like it! The layout remains the same, but everything else screams luxury – and good taste. And it's perfect for boys and girls!'

'Can you smell my Brut? No, but I can feel it against my leg ... It's here that Medallion Man takes off his tight trousers and tousles his chest hair.'

WHEN GOOD HOMES GO BAD # 12
THE 1970S MASCULINE BATHROOM

Before

Stuck in a Brut-smelling time warp, this, believe
it or not, is the dated bathroom of celebrated pop picker
and all-round good guy, Tony Blackburn. Probably no
surprise, then, to discover that, as with his bedroom
(see pages 194–197), it too is desperately in need of a
major update. The black tiles were probably a good idea
at the time, but hey – so was buying an Austin Allegro
and look what happed to them. Aye – it's time for this
bathroom to flush out the past and bathe in
a brighter future . . .

'King of the Jungle – this bathroom's had a renaissance, just like Tony Blackburn's career.'

After

Smart, modern and downright sexy, this reborn bathroom now has a colour scheme that's both cool and calming. What's more, it's kitted out as an efficient space for the user. And with a loo as gorge as this, the only problem will be getting people to 'use it and move it' so that other family members can get on with their ablutions in the morning!

Mirrors

To make this small space feel much, larger we created an infinity effect by positioning mirrors opposite each other on either side of the bathroom. To make them an even greater architectural feature we had them pre-drilled to accommodate lighting, which we wired in from behind.

Practicality

A perfect room should be beautiful *and* practical, so we introduced beauty through colour and practicality via tiling. Very much in the style of a wet room, we tiled top to toe to guarantee the space remained leak-free and completely waterproof.

Space

We avoided a built-in shower cabinet and pedestal sink in favour of a spindly steel framework as this meant we didn't take up as much 'eye space'. The open-plan style looks cleaner too.

Colour scheme

Inspiration – just where does it come from? Well, it comes from a variety of places … you just have to open your eyes to it. Here we were inspired by the elegant packaging of Chanel Pour Monsieur, a timeless gentleman's fragrance that uses grey and white in its sophisticated packaging. If it's good enough for Coco Chanel, it's good enough for us!

Equipment

Before you rush out and purchase a new bathroom suite, think about what you need from your space and how you can make things easier for you and your family. Maybe a double sink could sort out you and your partner in the morning? Or perhaps a Jacuzzi bath could ease away stresses and strains at the end of a busy day? And just because you've installed a shower cubicle, don't think that an attachment over the bath isn't necessary! C'mon: how else can you wash your hair without getting everything else wet?

CONCLUSION: AN END TO BAD TASTE?

Phew! You've made it to our final chapter in one piece. The *How Not To Decorate* course of aversion therapy is almost complete. As we've clearly demonstrated, it's an ugly world out there but, via our guidance, you should be *almost* ready to cope. At this point you have two options. The first is to grab your 'good taste diploma' and shake it in the air for all to see as you denounce, once and for all, the evils of shag pile, stone cladding and woodchip. The second option is to dance with the devil in the magnolia-hued moonlight as you fall, once again, into the arms of extreme bad taste. Option one? Option two? Option one? Option two...?

To be *extra* sure we've cured you, we've assembled one final prescription to help you through those darkest moments. When kissing goodbye to any addiction, there'll be moments when your resolve will waiver. What you need at times like these are salient reminders of the horrors you've left behind. You should refer to our guide any time you feel alone, frightened or on the point of buying a Barbie toilet-roll holder or a shell-covered lamp base. You'll get there. You can do it. One day at a time...

Deadly design cocktails

Combine any of the following ingredients in your home, pour on liberal quantities of intoxicating bad taste, shake, stir ... then prepare to *gag*. It really is dangerously easy. To make sure your abode is a retch-free zone, you'd better listen up. Aye, here are some shocking examples of dire pairings that make the Krankies seem positively sophisticated:

 Walls and timber cladding. In any room. At any time. It's just WRONG. In fact it's blinkin' *criminal*.

 Pets and shag pile. Surprise, surprise, feline faecal deposits and canine urological issue in long-haired carpets are a total turn off. Either mow your carpet, shave your pussy, or pop your pooch into pop socks. And, for the love of God, make sure he pees in his box. Our gorgeous boy Felix wouldn't have it any other way ...

 Bathrooms and carpets. Yuk, yuk, and triple yuk. Do you *really* want to share your shower with a million billion bacteria? Thought not ...

 Tiles and wallpaper. One or the other is enough. Trust us. Remember The Grand Dunce, sorry DAME of Decorating Disaster, aka Christine Hamilton. 'Nuff said ...

 Horrid orange pine and human life. Why would you ever want to mix the two?

 Velvet shell-backed sofas and velour scallop-edged cushions – in ANY colour. They'll drive you mental in the long run, though you're clearly on the way already if you're buying this kind of stuff.

 Frilly café-style net curtains set against leaded glass windows. Beelzebub's own screening.

 Nylon 'satin-style' sheets with nylon quilted bed shams. Sparks will fly if you team these two up. Who wants to get that kind of shock under the duvet?

Colour me fabulous

Let's just come out and say it: some of us simply weren't meant to look into the giant colour sample book of life and pick out a gorgeous scheme. Of course we were, but as for the rest of you? *Hmm*. So, to help you through a vile wilderness of lamentable lime green, bilious bubblegum pink and cat-sick orange, here are a few 'can't-fail' C and J colour suggestions.

The winners . . .

1 Chocolate-brown and caramel-beige. Delicious every time.

2 Mint-green and white. Fresh and calming and one of our personal faves.

3 Toffee-brown and burnt-umber red. Just like our very own Glasgow living room . . .

4 Silver and white. Easy to create and a guaranteed winner.

5 Khaki-green and soft gold. Mother Nature with a touch of indulgent spend . . .

6 Egyptian sandy yellow and moody jet black. Darlings, talk about contrast!

7 Amethyst purple and white – if, that is, you're *ultra* confident. If you're still finding your designer feet, tone things down a little and opt for lilac and white till you get the knack.

8 Bitter chocolate and cream. A softer take on monochrome.

. . . and the sinners

1 Terracotta and vibrant yellow. They might look good in the med, but in our climate? Eh, NO.

2 Brown and ANY primary colour. School's out. Forget it.

3 Red and blue. Each gorgeous in isolation . . . but when they marry? It's like a decorating divorce made in hell.

4 Lilac and green. We've seen it attempted on many occasions, but to desperate effect each time . . .

5 Vivid red and vivid green. Should never be seen, etc., etc., etc.

6 Purple and orange. WE'LL decide when it's time for a 70s revival.

7 Turquoise and pink. No. No. No. And no again.

8 Navy blue and burgundy. Fab as a bruise – but lousy at home.

Stop. Breathe. Put away the credit card.

Remember! Even when the sale siren's on red alert and fabulous bargains beckon, you've got to exercise restraint because *less is (generally) much much more*. Especially when it comes to trolls and other similar devil dolls. So step away from the porcelain pig! Ditch that gaudy gonk! And put down that scary china doll once and for all, 'cos it's all too easy to go overboard and end up with one (or even a hundred) too many . . .

Here are some collections to dodge . . .
(yes, we know we've talked collections already,
but a good point is worth making twice.)

1 Small 'cutesy' animal figures. YOU might deem them collectible: but we deem them disastrous. So get busy! Bin the ducks, frogs, pigs, puppies and anything, for that matter, that simply collects dust.

2 Tiny 'crystal' ornaments. Ok, so you might have spent a fortune on five star just to bolster your collection, but why bother? These lead-free petrol pets are a joke.

3 Toby jugs. Are for mugs. 'Nuff said.

4 Fairies and Dragons. If you don't know why, well, it's time for your design lobotomy.

5 Novelty tea towels/aprons/oven gloves/ mugs. 'Novelty', in design terminology, is equal to 'utter evil'.

Wait! Screw that! Flex your plastic again – it's time to blow the budget!

Sometimes you need to re-mortgage your homestead just to fill it with gorgeous things, but it can SO be worth it; the right purchase, after all, will bring you joy and happiness for a lifetime. Or will at least make your home look fantastic … which is what it's all about, *n'est pas*? Aye, some sound investments now could see your style stock going up, up and away:

 A well-made, solid dining table in light wood. The sort of table your kids can still sit around in fifty years' time and contest your will into the wee small hours.

 Simple but beautifully designed bathroom utilities. Remember, it's not just your own taste which you have to consider but those of future buyers. Avocado green may float your boat but we'd advise hanging on to a life-raft too …

 Avoid the cheap seduction of UVPC windows. You'll SO regret it. Opt instead for something much more subtle and understated. Something that's less of a giant shiny nightmare. Like timber.

How to tell if the world has moved on, and you quite clearly haven't . . .

If you're guilty of allowing any of the following dirty little thoughts into your brain, then it's time to lather, rinse and repeat until you're free of last century's design drudgery. Didn't anyone tell you it's a new millennium out there?

'Traffic-light orange and mud-brown sound like the perfect colours for a bathroom suite.

Hmm. I'm tired of my wooden wall cladding. It must be time to slap on a new layer.

A beaded curtain in a doorway says, "Come in, pull up a bean bag, I'm a chilled-out dude, man".

If my valance doesn't match my curtains, pillows and nightie then I can't sleep for pure shame.

If there's a plain wall in my house, it's because I haven't yet had time to put up thirty-seven commemorative plates.'

SO, WHERE DO YOU GO FROM HERE?

Is it time for **confession** … or **suppression?** Are you strong enough to admit you want to change? Or will you be forever blinkered and consigned to a life within rooms such as the ones you've seen here? You must be feeling fragile (even damaged?) having run, kicking and screaming, through Britain's WORST interior desecrations. Hey – even WE feel distressed. We've tried to be strong on your behalf (God, we're such martyrs), but our stomachs STILL churn as we leaf our own pages and scan homes so desperately wrong they simply *had* to be put right. And, bloody hell; all *you* had to do, as you walked our literary path of domestic disgrace, was to sniff smugly about how right (or how wrong?) you got *your* place. *Hmm.*

For us, however, it's been REALLY tough; we've actually had to *visit* ALL the homes featured, then remind ourselves just how shocking each one was. And it's taken its toll. We're not sleeping (for fear of seeing the devastating details in our dreams) and we've been abandoned by our posse of stylish friends lest bad taste is contagious and we pass it on to them. God save us – it's been tough, at times, to tell it like it is. We've rubbed salt into our own wounds, but we had to; it's cathartic, after all. And as we've said before, 'If you tell the truth … you shame the "designer" devil'.

But come on! Our wee book wasn't all bad news. Sure, we unveiled the satanic evil that crawls the earth disguised as interior design, but we also showed salvation, damn it, in every single 'after' shot. So please –

take heed and seek a new life, via your colour charts. For fear of coming over all Tammy Fay Baker, we have to say that our evangelical design 'lesson' should be followed AT ALL TIMES. Virtually every home owner in front of whom we waved our sparkly wands agreed that their lives became better thanks to the *How Not To Decorate* experience.

Ok, there are one or two who, as we tore mercilessly at their awful avocado bathrooms, became suddenly style literate, demanding as they did even more from the project. And there were even those who questioned our designs. *Aha* – but we always had the most glorious trump card; when they got tricky we simply showed them the footage of how shockingly bad their homes *had* been before we set to work! But hey, even those who were less than appreciative of our team's hard work ended up with a MUCH better place to live as a consequence of our visit. As the saying goes; 'You can please some of the people all of the time, and all of the people some of the time, but …' Well, you know the rest.

And, talking of knowing 'the rest', we hope you now do. We'll meet you at the other end of your designer nightmare, where you'll live happily forever in a stylish new world with everything that's gorgeous. You'll smile at us when we pass in the street and we'll smile back as you wander into the distance with your Conran Store bags bursting at the seams with fabulous things. And we'll breath a sigh of relief knowing that our mission of decorative beautification is nearing completion. Thank you and goodnight. Perhaps our work is done. For now …

SELECTED RESOURCES

You're almost there: can you feel the grime of bad taste being washed out of every pore? You're beautiful, you're radiant, you're in touch with your inner design diva. The only thing to do now is go *shopping*.

With this handy list of stockists there really is *no* excuse now for an abhorrent abode ...

DIY stores

B&Q
www.diy.com
T: 0845 609 6688
F: 023 8025 7480

Focus DIY
www.focusdiy.co.uk
T: 0845 600 4244

Homebase
www.homebase.co.uk
T: 0845 077 8888

MFI
www.mfi.co.uk
T: 0800 028 0937

Wickes
www.wickes.co.uk
T: 0870 6089001

Contemporary sofas, tables and lighting

3D Upholstery
www.3dupholstery.co.uk
T: 0800 026 0715
T: 01384 567101

Aarrow Fires
www.aarrowfires.com
T: 01308 427234
F: 01308 423441

Aquaplus Solutions
Bathroom utilities and accessories
www.aquaplussolutions.com
T: 0870 201 1915
F: 0870 201 1916

Argos
Radiator covers
www.argos.co.uk
T: 0870 600 8784

Au Naturale
Textiles and accessories
www.aunaturale.co.uk

Bathroom City
www.bathroomcity.co.uk
sales@bathroomcity.com
T: 0121 753 0700
F: 0121 753 1110

Belgica Furniture
www.belgicafurniture.com
info@belgicafurniture.com
T: 01506 829 447
F: 01506 829 231

Bensons Beds
www.bensonsforbeds.co.uk
T: 01303 220 871

Bhs
www.bhs.co.uk
T: 020 7262 3288

Brabantia
Kitchen accessories
www.brabantia.com
info.uk@brabantia.com

Caple
Kitchen units and appliances
www.caple.co.uk
T: 0870 606 9606

Christopher Wray
Lighting
www.christopher-wray.com
sales@christopherwray.com
T: 020 7751 8701
F: 020 7751 8699

Colonial
Furniture
www.colonial.uk.com
T: 0131 557 5711

Connections Interiors
Blinds
www.connections.uk.net
T: 01702 470 939

Cotswold Company
Bathroom accessories
www.cotswoldco.com
T: 0870 241 0973

Debenhams
www.debenhams.com
T: 0845 6 099 099

De Dietrich
Kitchen utilities
www.dedietrich.co.uk
www.branduk.com
T: 0870 060 3230

De'longhi
Electric fires
www.delonghi.co.uk
T: 0845 600 6845

Dimplex
Electric heating
www.dimplex.co.uk
T: 0870 077 7117
F: 0870 727 0102

DK Heating
Underfloor heating
www.floorwarmingcompany.co.uk
T: 01895 825288

Dreams to Themes
Furniture
www.dreams-to-themes.co.uk
T: 01709 867428

Dualit
Kitchen accessories
www.dualit.com
info@dualit.com
T: 01293 652500

Dunelm Mill
Soft furnishings
www.dunelmmill.com
T: 0116 264 4400
F: 0116 264 4459

Duravit
Bathroom utilities and accessories
www.duravit.com
info@uk.duravit.com
T: 0870 730 7787

Elizabeth Stewart Design
Soft furnishing and accessories
www.elizabethstewart.co.uk
T: 020 8440 6363

Expert Bed Company Ltd
www.expert-bed-company.co.uk
mail@expert-bed-company.co.uk
T: 0870 766 8492

Fast Frames
Picture frames
www.fastframes.co.uk
T: 0871 550 0031

FCI
Furniture
www.fci.uk.com
info@fci.uk.com
T: 0870 774 1335

Flamingbox
Sound and vision technology
www.flamingbox.com
T: 01985 845 440

Flexa Furniture Ltd
www.flexa.dk
five@flexa.dk
T: 01223 840 800

Furniture Village
www.furniturevillage.co.uk
T: 01753 897700

George Maxwell
Sofas
www.georgemaxwell.com
sales@georgemaxwell.com
T: 01204 399397
F: 01204 433985

Habitat
www.habitat.net
T: 0845 6010740

Halo
Leather sofas
www.halo.co.uk

Hansgrohe
Bathroom utilities and accessories
www.hansgrohe.co.uk
insales@hansgrohe.co.uk
T: 0870 770 1972

Hillary's Blinds
www.hillarys.co.uk
T: 0800 916 6524

Homes in Heaven
Furniture
www.homesinheaven.net
T: 020 7736 2227
F: 020 7736 2272

House of Fraser
www.houseoffraser.co.uk
T: 0870 606 1010

Hotpoint
Kitchen appliances
www.hotpoint.co.uk
T: 08701 506070

Ikea
www.ikea.com
T: 0845 355 1141

Indigo Furniture
www.indigofurniture.co.uk
sales@indigofurniture.co.uk
T: 01629 581800

John Lewis
www.johnlewis.com
T: 020 7828 1000

Lakeland
Kitchen accessories
www.lakelandlimited.co.uk
T: 01539 488100

Laura Ashley
Soft furnishings
www.lauraashley.com
T: 0871 230 2301

Le Creuset
Kitchen accessories
www.lecreuset.co.uk
helpline@lecreuset.co.uk
T: 0800 37 37 92
F: 01264 354 403

Lightsaver
Lighting
www.lightsaver.co.uk
T: 0121 350 1999

Marks and Spencer
Lighting
www.marksandspencer.com
T: 0845 609 0200

Natuzzi
Contemporary sofas, tables and lighting
www.natuzzi.co.uk
T: 01322 312550

Newage Designs
Contemporary furniture
www.newage-living.com
T: 0161 832 7308

Next
www.next.co.uk
T: 08703 435 435

Nights In Iron
Iron beds and furniture
www.nightsiniron.com
sales@nightsiniron.com
T: 020 7636 6866
F: 020 7636 4554

Nono
Fabric for soft furnishings
www.nono.co.uk
T: 01565 757400

Porcelanosa
Kitchens, bathrooms and ceramic tiles
www.porcelanosa.co.uk
T: 0800 915 4000

QVS Direct
Electrical fixtures and fittings
www.qvsdirect.co.uk
T: 01342 844 094

Raft
Furniture
www.raftltd.co.uk
T: 020 8450 5078
F: 020 8450 5233

Range Master
Cookers and accessories
www.rangemaster.co.uk
T: 0870 789 6110

Rosco Bathrooms
www.bathroomheaven.com
jonathan@roscobathrooms.co.uk
T: 01934 712299
F: 01934 713222

Rosebys
Soft furnishings
www.rosebys.co.uk
webenquiries@rosebys.com
T: 0800 052 0493

Scumble Goosie
*Ready-to-paint and
hand-painted furniture*
www.scumble-goosie.co.uk
T: 01453 731305

Select Lighting
www.washington-lc.co.uk
T: 0800 013 3363

Smeg
Kitchen utilities
www.smeg.com
customer.service@smeguk.com
T: 0870 9909907
F: 01235 828330

Sofa Workshop Direct
www.sofaworkshop.com
T: 01798 343400

Tesco
www.tesco.com
T: 0870 6076060

The Accessory Store
Bathroom accessories
www.accessorystore.net
T: 01702 716 655

The Artistic Blind Company
www.artisticblinds.co.uk
T: 0117 910 9888

The Chair
www.thechair.co.uk
T: 020 7091 1199

The Couch Potato Company
Furniture and accessories
www.couchpotatocompany.com
info@couchpotatocompany.com
T: 020 8894 1333
F: 020 8894 1888

The Radiator Company
www.theradiatorcompany.co.uk
sales@theradiatorcompany.co.uk
T: 08707 302250

TK Maxx
Homeware accessories
www.tkmaxx.com
T: 01923 473367

Typhoon
Kitchen accessories
www.typhooneurope.com
info@typhooneurope.com
T: 020 8974 4755

Viva Sofas
www.vivasofa.co.uk
T: 01798 343400

West One Bathrooms Group
www.westonebathrooms.com
T: 020 7720 9333

Woolworths
Candles, crockery and accessories
www.woolworths.co.uk
T: 0870 333 711

Paint and Wallcoverings

Crown
Paints
www.crownpaint.co.uk
T: 0870 2401127

Dulux
Paints
www.dulux.co.uk
T: 01753 550555

Graham and Brown
Innovative wallpaper
www.grahambrown.com
T: 0800 328 8452

Johnstone's
Paints
www.johnstones-paints.co.uk
T: 01924 354000

Kalon
Paints
www.kalon.com
T: 01924 354500
F: 01924 354501

Neisha Crosland
Wallpaper
www.neishacrosland.com/
T: 020 7584 7988

Osborne and Little
Wallpaper
www.osborneandlittle.com
showroom@osborneandlittle.com
Tel: 020 7352 1456
Fax: 020 7351 7813

Sandersons
Paints
www.sanderson-online.co.uk
T: 01895 830 044

Smith & Wareham
Mosaic tiles
www.smithandwareham.co.uk
T: 01284 704 188

Surface
Tiles
www.surfacetiles.com
info@surfacetiles.com
T: 020 7819 2300

Timorous Beasties
Contemporary and traditional wallpaper
www.timorousbeasties.com
T: 0141 337 2622

Topps Tiles
www.toppstiles.co.uk
T: 0800 783 6262

Flooring

Allied Carpets
www.alliedcarpets.co.uk
T: 08000 932 932

Amtico Flooring
www.amtico.com
T: 0121 745 0800

Crucial Trading
Carpets
www.crucial-trading.com
T: 01562 743747

Flooring Supplies
www.flooringsupplies.co.uk
T: 0871 250 1066

Kahrs
Flooring
www.kahrs.com
info@kahrs.se
T: +44 1 243 778 747
F: +44 1 243 531 237

Karndean Flooring
www.karndean.com
T: 01386 820100
F: 01386 761249

Kersaint Cobb
Carpets
www.kersaintcobb.co.uk
sales@kersaintcobb.co.uk
T: 01675 430430
F: 01675 430222

Kristoffersen Carpets
www.kristoffersencarpets.com
T: 0131 454 0879

Pergo
Laminate flooring
www.pergo.com
T: 0800 374 771

Woodline Floors
Oak flooring
www.woodlinefloors.co.uk
T: 08708 408484

Made-to-Measure

Barking Mad & Co
Bespoke prints
www.barkingmadandco.com
T: 01625 524805

Custom Images Ltd
Bespoke canvases and wallpaper
www.customimages.co.uk
T: 0169 747 2522

Fraser James
Fitted kitchens
www.heartoftheshires.co.uk/fraserjames
T: 01327 315037
T: 07947 472416

GX Signs
Neon signs
www.signage.co.uk
T: 01273 597799

Jali Ltd
Radiator covers and bespoke furniture
www.jali.co.uk
sales@jali.co.uk
T: 01227 833 333
F: 01227 831 950

KBA Direct Ltd
*Kitchen and bedroom
designers and fitters*
www.kbadirect.com
info@kbadirect.com
T: 01895 820 204

Manhattan Furniture
Kitchen designers and builders
www.manhattan.co.uk
manhattan@manhattan.co.uk
T: 01903 524 300
F: 01903 750 679

Now Kitchens
Bespoke kitchens
www.nowkitchens.co.uk
T: 01772 703838
F: 01772 705788

Opus Stained Glass
www.opusstainedglass.co.uk
T: 01273 857 223

Pop Art Plastic
Pop Art wall tiles
www.popartplastic.co.uk
T: 01227 709 775

Symphony Group
Fitted wardrobes and fitted kitchens
www.symphony-group.co.uk
T: 0870 120 8000

For further details of suppliers used in
the *How Not To Decorate* series, please
see the Five website at www.five.tv.

ACKNOWLEDGEMENTS

For my late father Dan who I miss every day. Thank you, simply, for being. And for my mum Claire, my sisters Colette and Carmel, and my big brother Damian. I hope you've all enjoyed this crazy journey. And for Felix, Britain's biggest celebrity pussy … who gets double the hugs now Winnie's wearing his little ginger wings. And for Colin, who's put up with me through thick and thin for the last TWENTY years – thanks for everything you've given me. *Love Justin xx*

Thanks to my mum, Trudi, whose energy and vitality never fails to amaze me. To Felix – a feline firefighter and fluffy friend. And to Justin for fun, friendship and a whole lot more! *Colin xx*

We'd both like to thank the following:

To Ben Frow for your belief in the *grotesque*. Thanks for your guidance, support and friendship … and for introducing us to Bourbon Sours. We are forever in your debt. May Ireland be all you hope it to be.

To Dan Chambers, Walter Iuzzolino, Emma Derrick, Michelle Wales and everybody at Five. Thanks also to Louise Plank, Natasha Mensah, Stephanie Faber and all at Picture Publicity.

To Jo Ball, Simon Toyne and all the gang at Ricochet Productions. And to all the camera and sound crews that captured everything so perfectly.

To all our design assistants, but especially the wondrous Katie Sheffer. Thanks for the drama and the glamour. We love you all to bits, through ALL the tears. Aye, that's yours AND ours!

To Sue and Sue and the team at Knight Ayton Management – thank you for your navigation and inspiration. And for teaching us when to say 'no'.

To the HN2D builders – Andy (the most miserable, yet strangely fabulous builder in Britain), Dickie, Stuart, Paul the pocket rocket and Marcus.

To Alison Griffin and all at Lake Smith Griffin Associates for keeping the press fires burning. And of course for showing us the bigger picture.

To Antonia Hodgson, our editor at Time Warner. Thanks for 'getting' our message and for all those glossy restaurants (any excuse, huh?) as we planned this bad taste bible. Thanks for all the fun, the laughter and all that Champagne. And thanks simply for being so fabulous . . .

To Caroline Hogg for her bad taste supply. We know it's all yours really. Thanks also to David Young, Ursula Mackenzie, Rob Manser, Alison Lindsay, Rebecca Gray, Kirsteen Brace, Marie Hrynczak and everyone at Time Warner – the veritable von Trapps of publishing. You came to our book auction team-handed and we SO loved that.

To Emma, Alex, Katrin, Jess (!) and all at Smith & Gilmour for making BAD taste look so GOOD. Oh, and thanks for all those fabulous barbecues on your terrace!

Thanks to Tom Howard, Marcia Stanton (and her assistant Inca Bayer) and Ian Mackintosh for the photography, styling and make-up. Thanks, darlings, for gilding the C and J lily. We couldn't ask for nicer people to share a near-death (remember the ladder trauma?) experience with.

Thanks also to Luigi Bonomi for making things happen.

And not forgetting all at DMG World Media, Debby, Brian and Robyn; John Amabile; Amanda Lowe, Jeanette Burns, Sally Howitt, Philip Macfarlane, Fhiona Macka; Peter Samson and William Irons; Kelly Cooper-Barr; Elaine and George Ponte; Maureen Dunlop, Zora Sulema and Stephanie Blanc 'et ses parents' in France who lent us their wonderful Biarritz home to cross the t's and dot the i's in this book . . .

Thanks to Beverly Brown for that first SMG career opportunity all those years back. Thank you, also, to Liz Cowan, Alan Rennie and everyone at *Right at Home* and the *Sunday Mail* newspaper; to the *Sunday Mirror*; the *Birmingham Post*; the *Newcastle Journal*; the *Cardiff Western Mail*, the *Liverpool Daily Post*; *Uptown* magazine and *Reveal* – all of whom carry our columns.

To Glasgow. For being the best city in the world. You gave us the drive, the encouragement and all the support we needed to leave . . . and then come back. We're so proud to be citizens of *The Dear Green Place*.

And finally for our wonderful friend Grahame McGowan who babysits our best boy Felix as we go off on our travels. We thank you; your support has been amazing.